Family Business:
A Survival Guide

Family Business:
A Survival Guide

Kieran McCarthy

Chartered
Accountants
Ireland

Published in 2014 by
Chartered Accountants Ireland
Chartered Accountants House
47–49 Pearse Street
Dublin 2
www.charteredaccountants.ie

ISBN 978-1-908199-77-5

Typeset by Datapage
Printed by CPI Group (UK) Ltd, Croydon, CR0 4YY

To my mum and dad, Des and Theresa McCarthy,
who taught me that family and business could be compatible and
gave me an excellent grounding in both.

Contents

Acknowledgements

I would like to thank Philip Smyth, who mentored me in writing this book and who first gave me the idea and inspiration for it.

I would also like to thank Chartered Accountants Ireland for publishing this book, in particular the publishing team, headed by Director of Publishing, Michael Diviney. Thank you for your support during the writing process.

I am grateful to the very busy entrepreneurs who agreed to be interviewed for this book: Darina Allen (Ballymaloe), Marian O'Gorman (The Kilkenny Group), Patrick Buckley (EPS Group), Siobhan Browne (Siobhan Browne and Associates Limited), Michael Dickson (M I Dickson) and Alex Polizzi (Forte Hotel Group). Their contribution was essential in providing insights into life on the coalface of family businesses.

To my sister Shona and brothers Niall and Eoin, who have been a great source of inspiration and support throughout my life.

Many thanks to my colleagues at Hughes Blake for their support and interest in my work. They make office life enjoyable and stimulating. Thanks also to Caroline Lane, who typed drafts of the manuscript.

Thanks to the Tuesday organised play members of the Fitzwilliam Lawn Tennis Club, who are friends off-court and admirable foes on-court.

Finally, for her constant support and care, thank you to Celia Healy.

The Fascination and Frustration of the Family Business

A reader might wonder why this book is necessary – aren't there enough business books out there to satisfy demand? It is certainly the case that business books are an industry in themselves, but what I found was that there was no dedicated book to guide the family business on the advantages and disadvantages it has and will face in its bid to create a sustainable business for future generations. As an accountant specialising in family business, I'm aware of the resources available and I recognised that there was a need for an expert view of this business model that would explain in detail the myriad complexities that make the family business so frustrating and yet so fascinating.

First, what is a family business? This book defines it as any business where the owner-manager or his or her family owns more than 50% of the voting shares, or any enterprise where the owner or his or her family can appoint the management and decide which direction the enterprise should take. Family businesses are unique within the business world, and each family business is unique in itself. They differ from their corporate counterparts in their advantages and disadvantages. The advantages include long-term sustainability, faster decision making, strong work ethic and values, strong community ties and supplier/staff relationships. The disadvantages include negative perceptions of family business, nepotism, potential for damaging personal as well as professional conflict, less access to cash than quoted companies, resistance to change and pressure on family members to join the company. It takes a strong family and a strong business sense to negotiate these challenges effectively and create an enterprise that can be passed from generation to generation.

In spite of the challenges, the family business accounts for 75% of all business in Ireland, which means it is a hugely influential and powerful business model. This book examines all of the key aspects of that model, describing the many pitfalls that can undermine a business and giving advice and tips on how best to manage, plan and conduct the business. The facts, figures and discussions are complemented by interviews with owners of successful family businesses – such as Darina Allen, Marian O'Gorman, Alex Polizzi, Michael Dickson and Patrick Buckley – who give important and useful insights into how a family businesses can thrive or fail. It is a complete and thorough assessment that will prove a valuable handbook to all those who own, work in, or are thinking about joining, a family business.

How to Succeed in Family Business

Naturally, there is no simple formula that will fit all businesses, but it is possible to identify four factors that all successful family businesses share: good communication; a values-led culture; a clear, well-described vision; and careful and conscientious stewardship of the entire enterprise. In order to establish these four cornerstones of the business, it requires a sustained and concentrated input from the owning family to set up the policies, documents and frameworks necessary for the business to be transparent, ethical in all dealings and essentially well-run.

Again and again, successful family business owners emphasise the importance of ongoing and effective communication at all levels of the enterprise, with input from all staff encouraged, accommodated and heard. They also highlight the importance of a distinct, cohesive and reliable set of values by which to do business, which is essentially a top-down culture that benefits and enhances the business in all its workings. There is enormous responsibility on the owners and managers, and they need to acknowledge this and fully take it on board. In this way, the business will work within clearly set parameters that provide an internal regulation and assessment system that benefits everyone.

The Question of Governance

Part II is devoted to the issues surrounding family governance and corporate governance. These two areas are treated separately, but they work together to inform how the business is operated, its rules and overarching framework. The benefits, means and outcomes of professionalisation are laid out clearly, with lots of tips and advice on how to ensure that the family business is operating to its full potential in a modern, progressive and inclusive manner. When dealing with family members, it might be tempting to have a more easy-going, ad hoc approach to business dealings, but in fact a family business, by virtue of its make-up, needs strong governance structures to ensure fairness, equality, accountability and transparency at every level.

Naturally, a family business is open to accusations of favouritism and 'keeping it in the family', so for all concerned it is essential that the governance processes are open to examination and 100% consistent for all staff and managers. In this case, size doesn't matter at all – even a very small family business will benefit from having in place structures that promote fair dealings and protect the interests of all involved. It is the business of every managing family to take all necessary steps to ensure that conflict and contentious issues are dealt with and resolved swiftly, fairly and always to the benefit of the business.

Women in Business

There has been a significant overhaul of attitudes and practices in recent times with regard to the role of women in the family business. This is an interesting aspect of the sector and it is good to see that the family business is now in the vanguard of change, with increasing involvement by female family members, right up to CEO and owner level. This is to be welcomed, as all the research conducted on this topic supports the contention that women are a beneficial addition to business, bringing an important dimension of professionalism and lateral thinking to the boardroom table. Interviews with successful women, such as Darina Allen of Ballymaloe, Marian O'Gorman of Kilkenny Group (see **Chapter 9**) and Alex Polizzi of the Forte Hotel Group, showcase the ability and ambition of a new generation of owners, giving a very clear view of what the future holds for 'daughters' now that education is widely accessible and women are valued equally for their abilities. It is a welcome new chapter in the story of the family business and one that is important to applaud and encourage.

Succession

There are many issues for a family business to contend with, but generally it is succession that throws up the greatest challenges. The statistics are sobering and sound a very clear warning note: one in three family business fail within the first three years; less than 30% of family firms (40% in the US) make it to the second generation; only 10% (13% in the US) of those succeed to the third generation. It is clear, then, that succession is something to be handled with great care. Accordingly, this book discusses this issue in depth, starting with Ivan Lansberg's excellent advice that 'succession is a process, not an event' and moving on to describe how every party to that process should plan for succession in a sensible, informed and coordinated way that takes into account the professional and the personal aspects affecting that succession. The aim of this section of the book is to provide a working blueprint for how to set up the systems that will enable effective transfer of the business from one generation to the next.

An Invaluable Guidebook

It would be fair to say that the term 'family business' is not always favourably viewed in Ireland. We have a strange relationship with the notion of a business owned and run by a family – on the one hand, it inspires trust and brand loyalty; on the other hand there is a tendency to see a 'family business' as a lesser operation than a multinational or large corporate entity. This view is certainly not supported by the facts and figures, such as we have them. Family businesses make up 75% of all enterprises in Ireland and account for 50% of employment in the private sector, contributing hugely to jobs, the local economy, social cohesion, export business and national charity funding/sponsorship. If the Irish family business sector collapsed in the morning, the backbone of the country would be gone, and the entire economic system would collapse in the same moment. The truth is that the family business in Ireland is essential to the economic well-being and stability of the whole country.

It is from this position that I set out to capture both the 'small picture' and the 'big picture' of the Irish family business – from a position of admiring those who work so hard to create and sustain family enterprises, from having first-hand experience of the family business through my parents' enterprises and from working very closely with family businesses of all types through my work as a specialist accountant to such businesses.

I engage with the family business model at all levels and know intimately its fascinating make-up and its frustrating challenges and obstacles. This book is, then, an insider's look at the small-picture details such as interpersonal dynamics, and the big-picture essentials such as succession and governance. It sets out to provide all those interested in this area with a solid overview of the model and a solid understanding of how *not* to run a family business, and how to run a good, viable and sustainable family business that brings pride and prosperity generations into the future.

Kieran McCarthy
August 2014

Part I

The Entrepreneur and the Family

CHAPTER 1

The Strengths and Weaknesses of Family Businesses

What is a Family Business?

Family businesses differ from non-family businesses in a number of important ways, and these differences can be critical to their success or failure. These differences, or 'dynamics', must be clearly understood by the owners and management in order to successfully negotiate both the opportunities and challenges they present.

For the purposes of this book, a 'family business' is defined as any business where the owner-manager, or his or her family, owns more than 50% of the voting shares, or any enterprise where the owner or his or her family can appoint the management and decide which direction the enterprise should take. When asked, "What makes a business a family business?", one wise advisor responded: "When an entrepreneur gets married, a family business is born."

In psychological terms, 'family dynamics' is the pattern of interactions within a family. It refers to the family make-up, the individual roles and how these affect each member. In terms of the family business, it is necessary that family members and those working in the company understand how these patterns inform and affect the business, its objectives and its future.

Of course, there is no single, set pattern that applies to all families. Each family business, just like each family, is unique. However, an understanding of family dynamics can allow patterns to be identified, which can assist the owner-manager in avoiding the mistakes made by other family businesses.

The most common mistakes made by the family business entrepreneur include: not planning early enough for succession; assuming the next generation will have the same passion and drive as the first generation; and not seeking guidance on exit strategy, which is a thorny area given that the first generation must somehow, usually reluctantly, 'let go' of the business. These and other issues will be covered in depth over the course of this book.

Family Business Sectors

Although family businesses are found in every sector of the economy in Ireland, there are particular sectors towards which they appear to gravitate. The sectors that seem to be a natural fit for family business are:

- **Retail and distribution:** for example, the Dunne family operates the very successful chain of Dunnes Stores, the Musgrave family operates the SuperValu franchise, Superquinn was a well-known family business until recently and Smyth's Toys is a first-generation family business.
- **Hotels, hospitality, and catering:** dominated by the Doyle, Fitzpatrick, Ryan, Jury and O'Callaghan families, to name but a few. It is interesting to note that most hotels in Ireland and across the world are family-owned.
- **Food processing:** for example, the Goodman, Carton, Queally, Brennan and McCarron families.
- **Car dealerships:** family names like O'Flaherty, Flanagan, Keane, Gowan and Boland are prominent in this sector.

Sectors where there is good cash flow appear to attract family businesses. Family businesses also tend to do well in sectors in which the owner-management aspect is important.

The Advantages of Being a Family Business

I will examine the challenges facing the family business below, but suffice to say there are significant challenges in setting up and running of this type of business operation. This is borne out in the fact that only 10–30% of family businesses survive to the third generation, even though approximately 75% of all Irish businesses are family-owned and account for more than 50% of both Ireland's GDP and its workforce.[1]

So why, then, do so many Irish entrepreneurs choose to adopt this business model? The answer to that lies in the advantages of operating a family business.

NATURAL STRENGTHS OF FAMILY BUSINESSES

1. Coherent sense of purpose
2. Long-term sustainability
3. Faster decision making
4. Competitive advantage
5. Less risk-taking
6. Strong work ethic
7. Family values
8. Strong community ties and supplier/staff relationships

1. Family businesses have a coherent sense of purpose

The established relationships and camaraderie between family members, and indeed with other family firms, can create a shared vision, strategic unity and a sense of partnership not available to non-family businesses. Forthcoming generations are exposed early to pride in and passion for the business, which means the key members of the company are hugely invested in it, personally and commercially, and they work hard to secure its future.

While the potential for conflicting agendas and viewpoints among the different generations may be higher for family firms, at the same time families are natural teams and bring a unique sense of unity. In business, the team is everything. Teams work together towards a common goal, for a common good; people deliver value and are a company's most important asset. A strong team of talented people who share a common vision and have complementary skills is vital for building a successful enterprise.

[1] See "Taoiseach launches DCU Centre for Family Business", *Business and Leadership*, 10 October 2013, www.businessandleadership.com.

The importance of teamwork and having the 'right people' is especially true when building a business for future generations, which at some point will require taking a step back from working 'in' the business to working 'on' it. As David Molian of the Cranfield School of Management points out:

> "Unless you can recruit, retain and motivate talented people, you will never buy yourself the time to free yourself from doing the operational stuff. That has to come first. That will then allow the owner-manager to spend a significant amount of time in creating and fashioning the business tomorrow."[2]

When a family pulls together in this way, it can produce strong forward momentum. "I succeed when my family succeeds" is an old saying that applies to successful business families – the current generation strives to improve and grow the business for the sake and benefit of the next. It's a 'big picture', longer-term vision of truly responsible stewardship, one that can be embraced by all employees, who, together with the family, will focus on developing the business to make it sustainable – not just to look good at the next board meeting, but to make it strong for the foreseeable future. Ultimately, the goal of creating a successful family business that provides for the family into the future is a very strong incentive and a powerful motivator.

An emphasis on sustainable stewardship is a prerequisite for successful family firms, as illustrated in the example of A.J. & R.G. Barber Limited below.

EXAMPLE: A.J. & R.G. BARBER: A SHARED VISION[3]

A.J. & R.G. Barber Limited is a family business that has been making cheese for 180 years. The company has succeeded through six generations and it is now operated by four sixth-generation cousins, based in the same village in Somerset where the company was founded in 1833.

---

[2] Quoted in Rigby, G., *People Management for Entrepreneurs* (Harriman House, 2011).

[3] Giles Barber interviewed in Bridge, R., "We must learn from values behind success of family firms". *The Daily Telegraph*, 2 March 2013.

The company has an annual turnover of £70 million, employs 220 people and still makes its cheddar cheese to the original recipe. Counting Harrods, Fortnum & Mason and the main supermarket chains among its customers, this is an exceptionally successful family business.

Commercial Director Giles Barber believes that the success has a lot to do with being family-owned:

"Running a family business gives you a real sense of purpose. It is much more than just achieving a set of results at the end of a year. We have got a common goal to improve the business for the next generation as well as our own."

That shared vision is also adopted by non-family employees and suppliers. "We have generations of other people's families that have worked for the business and the 120 farms that supply their milk to our operation are all small farming businesses."

A special synergy of powerful forces can be created when family and business visions are brought together. With an amplified sense of purpose, mutual 'win–win' feelings and consequential commitment, wealth can be created and success sustained for future generations. The result is an ingrained culture of passion, loyalty and commitment towards a common purpose.

That said, while family dreams and business ambitions may be brought together successfully, they must also be kept distinct and separate enough to ensure that emotional issues do not affect commercial sensibility (for more on this, see **Chapter 2**). Equally, just as unity should be celebrated, it must not come at the expense of individuality, which should be nurtured and respected (see **Chapter 3**).

The point is that being part of a family team can make it easier to be passionate about the purpose of the business. As such, family firms should compel the generations to create visions that reach one step beyond profitability and short-term gain. These family-led visions stretch from generation to generation, forgoing immediate gain in favour of long-term prosperity.

2. Family businesses have long-term sustainability

Many family firms are more robust than other types of private business. This was the conclusion reached by a Credit Suisse report in 2012,[4] which revealed that 60% of family firms in the UK reported revenue growth of 5% or more in 2011, with listed family companies outperforming the stock market by 8% over the five years 2007–2012. A report compiled by the Institute for Family Business concurs, noting that during the recession insolvency rates rose at a slower rate for family firms of all sizes than for non-family businesses.[5] Professor Jim Lee of Texas A&M University Corpus Christi has similarly found that family businesses have the potential to be more profitable than other types of business: his studies revealed that family-managed firms outperformed companies with non-family managers at the helm, even during recessions.[6] While it remains a challenging task to survive through numerous generations, family businesses are still a dominant and robust economic force.

The ability to plan long-term strategies and see the 'bigger picture' is an advantage enjoyed by many family businesses. Non-family firms are often driven by short-term gains and share price concerns, with a focus on raising the value of the company over the short term rather than raising the sustainability (and subsequent wider value) of the company over the long term. They make decisions and take risks according to those driving factors. By contrast, shareholders within a family business tend to be more patient and will not 'breathe down the necks' of the management team for dividends and quarterly results. Short-term results give way to long-term investments; urgent demands give way to a more seasoned understanding of the bigger picture. This approach breeds resilience and is a key reason why family firms often weather economic downturns while their counterparts sink.

---

[4]   Credit Suisse Research Institute, "Family businesses: Sustaining performance", September 2012.

[5]   Institute of Family Business, "The UK Family Business Sector: Working to grow the UK economy", November 2011.

[6]   Lee, J., "Family Firm Performance: Further Evidence" (June 2006) Vol. 19 No. 2 *Family Business Review*.

Patrick Buckley, second-generation Deputy MD of EPS Group,[7] neatly sums up the benefits of long-term thinking:

"For us, the key aspect of a family business we have is the ability to take a more long-term view. The shareholders will be patient in terms of growth and we have the ability to make decisions that are not short-term, they are medium- to long-term. We can take investment decisions or strategic decisions that are for the benefit of the company over a period of 5 to 10 years rather than 6 to 12 months because we're not worried about the share price next month. It allows us to make decisions that are better for the business long-term, and we don't need to – and certainly have no ambition to – leverage the company in any significant way, so we fully focus on investment and growth using our own resources in the main. There are plenty of challenges and opportunities, so it's a case of focusing on those and focusing on continuing to grow and develop the business in a very sustainable way. We also have the added advantage whereby family members will decide to reside in a new chosen market and support the long-term development strategy of the company."

In business, patience is most certainly a virtue. The key to creating a sustainable, steadily growing business is to reinvest profits consistently. In the non-family business, however, there is a pressing requirement to pay high dividends to shareholders, to provide a rapid return on investment (ROI) and to take bigger risks in order to reach key performance indicator (KPI) targets, which can effectively disable those firms from reinvesting in the business. That lack of reinvestment, that pressure to perform immediately and pay out promptly, that urgent need to reward shareholders and investors can strangle the business and dilute its success over time. Patience, reinvestment and steady growth are more viable ways to build a business.

3. Family businesses can engage in faster decision making

While the family business stance is generally a long-term one, this does not mean that the pace of growth or decision making is any slower.

---

[7] Buckley, P. Interview with author (July 2013). EPS Group is a water and wastewater treatment and pumping solutions company (www.epswater.ie).

It may be steadier due to reinvestment and retention of equity instead of seeking debt or equity funding, but it is not necessarily less competitive or progressive. In fact, being part of a natural team can have the knock-on effect of enabling things to be done quicker. "For us, we have the ability to make decisions very quickly. We're very adaptable, we're more agile," adds Patrick Buckley of EPS Group.

In business, where time is money, everything will inevitably take longer and cost more than you think it will. Yet in a competitive landscape, the need for speed can be vital, for example being first to market. Speed of decision making can therefore be a real advantage in family firms, where strong bonds arising from close relationships among decision makers, a less politicised process and less bureaucracy can help speed things up. This makes 'thinking big, acting small, failing fast and learning rapidly' much more possible.

4. Family businesses can enjoy competitive advantage

When a family team works in unison towards a common goal, there is unrivalled commitment in terms of sheer hard work and dedication, trust and passion, reinforced by family membership, which cannot be duplicated in non-family firms. The commitment is also related to a sense of pride in the product or service. This can give a competitive edge and be a key contributor to a positive brand image.

Consumers are becoming increasingly desensitised and resistant to brands as a result of over-marketing and brand overload, so brands with strong, clear values and purpose have a competitive advantage in many ways. Family businesses that are seen as 'authentic' and purposeful, and display their passion and values in a transparent, honest way, will be favoured. People can buy into such brands and stay loyal to them in the long term.

5. Family businesses are less likely to take risks

Stemming from their longer-term, lower-pressure approach to business, family firms tend to take on levels of debt that are manageable or even shun debt entirely (many opt to self-finance and reinvest their own profits rather than overburden themselves). This approach means that risks are considered carefully and decisions are well-informed, particularly when it comes to financing the business. It is because family firms are in it for the long haul that they are far less likely to borrow. Take R.J. Balson & Son, for example, members of the 'Tercentenarian Club', whose members run businesses that have survived for at least 300 years. R.J. Balson & Son is a family butcher based in Bridport, Dorset, which has survived across 25 generations, passing the business down through the ages to the eldest male heir. Richard Balson says: "I don't borrow money, in fact, I don't hand over any money to the bank except for a small monthly fee to use the plastic card machine."[8] This is a common sentiment among family firms, which tend to play things safer. After all, if your main focus is growth and reputation, to build a viable company to pass on to children, grandchildren and beyond, you are less inclined to take risks or to play fast and loose just to boost share value.

Patrick Buckley of EPS Group echoes this:

> "Certainly, if you wanted to highly leverage the company you could grow very quickly in a potentially unsustainable manner; whereas we can take a different view: grow using our own resources, grow at our own pace whilst still having an aggressive growth strategy, albeit from the perspective of not risking the business with a lot of debt. That's the view we've taken with EPS: we don't want to go leveraging the company excessively. It has a very strong balance sheet of €23 million, a very solid, robust business and it's something we can build on for growth and diversification, but at our own pace. Sustainable leveraging for sustainable growth is our preferred route."[9]

6. Family businesses have a strong work ethic

Being exposed to and involved in the family business from a young age – whether just hearing about it at the kitchen table, working for the business part time at weekends or witnessing the hard work put in by parents – can have a tremendously positive effect on the work ethic of second and third generations. If you see first-hand the trials and tribulations that your parent(s) experienced in running the business, you get a firm grounding in what it takes to provide for the family unit. It is a lifelong lesson in hard work, achievement,

[8] Wallop, H., "They're 300 years old and still in business". *The Telegraph*, 1 January 2013. See also www.rjbalson.co.uk.
[9] Buckley, P. Interview with author (July 2013).

dedication and passion. This is recognised by Alex Polizzi, presenter of BBC's *The Fixer* and *The Hotel Inspector* and heir to the Forte hotel empire:

> "I always wanted to be involved in my family business and it's made an incredible difference to me, because I was with people who were very good at what they did and who worked very hard. I always perceived that that was what I was going to have to do as well."[10]

7. Family businesses operate according to family values

Trust is absolutely vital in business, and it comes as the result of having an honest, open environment marked by healthy communication. Family members tend to trust each other, whereas third parties and members of non-family companies may require, for example, non-disclosure agreements (NDAs) and other confidentiality agreements. Additionally, family business members are more likely to be loyal due to stronger personal bonds and a more deep-rooted sense of purpose. Loyalty, the notion of sticking together through thick and thin (because blood is thicker than water, of course), can prove incredibly resilient and important when the going gets tough and obstacles must be overcome.

A deeply ingrained sense of integrity and honesty are core strengths of family firms. They can hold a business together through challenging times and can certainly empower the creation and maintenance of solid, stable, long-term relationships, both within the company and with external clients, suppliers, etc.

While individuals will have differing opinions, personalities and so on, it is likely that family members, coming as they do from the same 'stock', will share a common ethos and be able to agree on how things should be done or what the business should ultimately stand for. This shared set of values can be drawn upon to gain competitive advantage.

Naturally, coming from the same family does not predispose you to sharing the same ideals, values or even vision. There may well be opposing ambitions and disparate ideals. However, underlying those differences there is likely to be a shared pride and passion for the

---

[10] Polizzi, A. Interview with author (June/July 2013).

company, which can be built upon when discussing the business's overall values, vision and mission.

8. Family businesses have strong community ties and supplier/staff relationships

A sense of shared kinship can spread beyond the family. As well as tending to partner with other family firms, members of family-owned businesses often have strong links with the wider community and build lasting relationships with customers and suppliers in those communities. This personal approach to doing business is a winning formula; after all, "people buy from people".

This personal touch and the importance of interpersonal relationships also applies within the business itself. According to research conducted by Professor Jim Lee, family businesses often consider their employees as extended family members and are therefore more reluctant to make staff redundant during downturns, unlike non-family firms that may be quicker to reduce staff numbers. The family view taken is that the employees will be required again when the business turns, and keeping staff means there will be no training or recruitment costs incurred later on, and customers/clients will remain better managed in the long run.[11] Similarly, a report by the Coutts Institute[12] identifies the key strengths across 300 of Britain's most successful family firms. These include flexibility in decision making, the personal touch, honesty and integrity in business affairs, the family as a source of commercial strength and exceptional human resources practice.

The better a business looks after and cares for its staff, the more likely they are to respond in kind and perform to the best of their abilities. Within the family business, there is usually an emphasis on creating an enjoyable working environment because the workforce are integral to the company's success and future development, and it's important to retain them. In a family business, every effort is made to find the right professional level for each member of staff and to

[11] Lee, J., "Family Firm Performance: Further Evidence" (June 2006) Vol. 19 No. 2 *Family Business Review*.

[12] Coutts Institute, "Qualities and Strengths of Family Businesses: Key Findings from the Coutts Prize for Family Business 2005–2010".

encourage ongoing personal and professional development. There is no desire to employ the 'step up or step out' approach that some organisations use to progress staff through the ranks according to predefined timescales. The payoff is enhanced loyalty to the business, a higher level of productivity and lower staff turnover.

The Challenges of Being a Family Businesses

As well as the advantages enjoyed by family businesses, there are unfortunately a number of disadvantages as well; and while they apply to business in general, they do include some to which family businesses are particularly prone.

NATURAL WEAKNESSES OF FAMILY BUSINESSES

1. The need to prove oneself
2. Resistance to change
3. Succession
4. Less access to cash than quoted companies
5. Nepotism
6. Blurred boundaries: family getting in the way of business
7. Greater potential for conflict
8. Pressure to join the family firm

1. The need to prove oneself

Family members often need to be prepared to work twice as hard as other employees in order to earn respect and avoid being tarnished with the 'silver spoon' accusation. "There's no free ride," says Alex Polizzi. "I expected to be judged harshly and to be criticised mercilessly and that was good preparation."[13]

Evidently, family members must earn their stripes in order to be accepted by the entire workforce. Michael Dickson, managing director of M I Dickson, one of England's longest-standing pork butchers

---

[13]   Polizzi, A. Interview with author (June/July 2013).

and still owned and managed by the family who founded the business in 1953, agrees:

> "When I was 19 and had completed my A-Levels, I joined my sister (and mother) in the business. I had worked regularly over weekends and during holidays, and by the time I decided I wasn't going to university and that this was a life I wished to follow, I assumed everything would fall into place once I worked full time. Alas, it didn't turn out that way. We had a staff of about 35 and the routine chauvinism my mother and sister had to put up with after my father's death, I was to experience in spades: I was very young, inexperienced, still had everything to learn and no obvious route into the necessary structured learning. Knowledge was power, so information and training weren't really available to me and sometimes consciously withheld, so I had a fairly tough time trying to break down the barriers."[14]

2. Resistance to change

The stability of a family business is an advantage, but it can also lead to an inability to react positively to change. While family businesses often have the advantage of agility when it comes to decision making, some families can be averse to making changes for fear of breaking with tradition, which slows down reaction times and can lead to negative effects. For example, while staff loyalty is a good thing and a testament to the ethos of a family firm, it can also lead to difficulties if an underperforming member of staff is left in place because the decision to terminate seems impossible to take. Indecision or delay caused by resistance to change can lead to companies missing out on opportunities.

3. Succession

Decisions regarding succession and future management can be delayed due to perpetual patterns of behaviour and a resistance by the owner-manager to let go. Indeed, succession issues, compounded by resistance to change, are consistently among the biggest problems faced by

[14] Dickson, M. Interview with author (July 2013).

family businesses. The founder or owner-manager of the firm may fear letting go for a number of reasons (these reasons, and the best way to successfully plan for succession, are covered in detail in **Chapter 10**). Leaving it too late to plan succession, however, is guaranteed to stand in the way of growth. The main reason that fewer than 33% of family businesses survive the transition from one generation to the next is not that there is no interest from the younger generation in taking the helm, but rather the lack of succession planning and preparation. The younger generation should be given room and time to grow and develop their skills so that they can readily and confidently assume leadership when the time comes.

What owners of family firms *should* do is:

- encourage the management team, board of directors and family council (see **Chapter 10**) to make important decisions quickly and facilitate this behaviour in others;
- empower staff to provide feedback to expedite matters; and
- make succession planning a key priority well ahead of the actual transition of leadership from one generation to the next.

Tradition and change do not have to conflict. It is possible to honour tradition while making the changes required to keep pace with competitors and economic shifts. Traditions that have worked for a successful company, and have therefore remained in place, should not stand in the way of progress and change; they should evolve accordingly.

4. *Less access to cash than quoted companies*

Private family businesses, despite their longevity and solid track records, can find access to cash to be more limited than quoted companies. This can make it difficult to raise capital/liquidity. That said, not having easy access to outside investment can further instil a risk-averse avoidance of debt or equity funding and, although growth may take longer as a result, it can be a safer and more viable way to grow. By comparison, some of the largest and most powerful companies in the world were created by raising capital in the public markets. Oil companies, utilities and technology companies have all accessed the markets to fund their day-to-day operations and grow their businesses. By selling all or part of a business in a public offering, companies that go public receive an immediate influx of capital. Family companies are restricted to raising funds from within the family means, banks or by selling a portion of the company to a third party.

5. Nepotism

Some family firms (generally the ones that fail to survive) are guilty of nepotism and of putting the family first, no matter what the cost. In these cases, positions are given to relatives who are not necessarily the best candidates for the job, or family members and family shareholders receive higher salaries and dividends than non-family members. Nepotism adversely affects both family and non-family members and is a recipe for disaster when it comes to the health and vitality of the business. Unfair treatment and limited career progression impact on the morale and motivation of non-family staff members. Furthermore, nepotism will have a negative effect even for those who benefit from such preferential treatment – it creates a feeling of being entitled to have a job for life, regardless of abilities or work ethic, which leads to a destructive complacency.

In order to combat this, rules and accountability must be kept paramount in the family business. There must be clear rules, rights, responsibilities and boundaries in place that everyone in the company is required to follow, regardless of their 'status' in relation to the family. Furthermore, these rules and boundaries should be governed by a mixed management of family and non-family members. When this sort of clarity and accountability is achieved, it enables effective communication and promotes respect, enthusiasm and productivity whilst reducing conflict. For example, one such rule might state that people should be hired based on their actual capabilities, merits, experience and strengths, not simply because they are a member of the family. (The importance of such governance will be examined in **Chapter 5**.)

Nepotism disempowers all employees, both family and non-family, and has an adverse effect on the profitability and sustainability of the business. Talented non-family members of staff are easily lost this way, so it is important to provide ample opportunities for career growth to *all* staff. While it is likely that family members may occupy some of the leadership positions, it's critical that they do not occupy all leadership positions. It is vital in business to find the right mixture and balance of talent to stimulate growth, partly to fill the gaps in skills and experience and partly to get wide, varied and valued input from less emotional and more objective perspectives. (The importance of non-family management teams, board members and external advisors is explored in **Chapters 6** and 7.)

6. *Blurred boundaries: family getting in the way of business*

Just as it is important to find the right balance of talent from both within and outside of the family, it is crucial to find the right balance between family and business and a commonality between family goals and business goals. As families, we have a responsibility to nurture individual identities and independence, to encourage respect between one another and provide emotional support and guidance in order to raise well-balanced, decent and responsible adults. As businesses, we need to create a motivated team of well-trained and valued individuals and grow a balanced, viable and sustainable business.

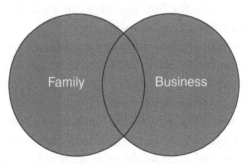

For the family business, there is an overlap between these two worlds that can result in blurred boundaries. Family and business are interconnected systems, but it is important to try to separate the two. One way to do this is to ensure that no family member directly manages another family member, as this can be fraught with complications, both personal and professional. From an employee perspective, getting criticism from anyone can be tough no matter how constructive it is; to receive it from a loved one can be even more difficult to deal with. On the other side, from a leadership point of view, emotions can get in the way of sound judgement when it comes to making business decisions. Again, balance is fundamental. When dealing with family members in a work environment, it is necessary to be sensitive enough not to cause problems at home, but fair and firm enough not to negatively affect the business.

7. Greater potential for conflict

Family relationships have long and often interesting histories, which makes them more emotive and less objective than non-family relationships. As such, the potential for conflict in family businesses can be greater than in non-family enterprises. As outlined above, there is an overlap between commercial business concerns and emotional family issues, so it is important to be able to separate business from personal lives during the working day. It is also vital to understand the interests and potentially disparate viewpoints and goals of each family member and to manage the dynamics of those relationships in order to minimise conflict.

Rivalries can spill over into the commercial environment, which is not good for business. There can also be issues around power and control, opposing views and poor communication between generations. At the same time, conflict can be flipped on its head to become a cause for positive change. If business leaders, family members, management and staff disagree on certain strategic points, this can be a useful opportunity to rethink the vision or strategy going forward.

It is important, however, to ensure that non-family members are not caught up in damaging family feuds. Many a talented team member has been lost after feeling like they were caught in the middle between family members in conflict. A hostile environment is never healthy. It is therefore important to have processes in place for handling conflict and to do everything possible to avoid it in the first place. Conflict in a family business is discussed in more detail in **Chapter 2**.

8. Pressure to join the family firm

Younger generations can feel pressured into joining the family firm. The weight of this responsibility can be hard to bear and leave them feeling trapped, as if joining the family firm might prevent them from pursuing their true ambitions.

Certainly, nobody should be forced into joining the firm or made to feel bad or inadequate for choosing not to do so. While it is important to provide attractive career opportunities for family members, the next generation should be free to pursue whatever career they wish.

They may never choose to join the firm or they may decide to join it once they've gained external experience. In fact, the latter is often preferred, as it gives younger family members an opportunity to prove themselves and gain experience outside the business, making them more valuable team members should they decide to come on board. The key word here is 'valuable' – a person who has been coerced or pushed into the family business is unlikely to become a pioneering staff member or leader. It is not wise to put short-sighted goals or 'wins' over another family member before the productivity and success of the business.

Exploiting the Advantages and Coping with the Challenges

The approximately 75% of family businesses that do not succeed through to the next generation are not necessarily failures. It could be that the first generation (e.g. a husband and wife team) do very well out of the business, but are unable to manage the transition process. This could mean freedom and the creation of liquidity for the next generation, opening up other opportunities and new paths to success that may not have been pursued had they taken the business forward. While transition from generation to generation is the ideal, this should only be pursued if the advantages of running and working for a family firm outweigh the challenges.

As we have seen in this chapter, building a successful family business is not just about profitability and turnover; it's also about the non-monetary things, the intangibles such as building strong, long-lasting relationships with employees, customers, suppliers and the community and creating loyalty, trust and respect. It's about seeing the bigger picture and long-term aims as well as the more immediate targets; growing at a speed that keeps that bigger picture in mind, reinvesting over the long term and being prudent when it comes to financing the business.

It's important to be adequately equipped for this journey, because that's what building a sustainable business viable enough to succeed through the generation is: a journey, not a race. Outlined below are the key things to consider as you set out or continue on this journey.

TIPS TO REMEMBER

1. **Be transparent and play to your strengths** Today's consumers are fast being desensitised to brands as a result of over-marketing and brand overload. In order to believe in brands, people want the truth – they want brands with a cause and a purpose. In today's 'rate me' culture, a company's reputation can be built or destroyed with a mere tweet or review. Thus, authentic, transparent, passionate brands and companies that have strong values and a clear purpose will be favoured. People can buy into such brands and stay loyal to them; they capture consumers' hearts and minds and create longevity. Family firms are perfectly positioned to take advantage of this and harness the power of their transparent, values-led, passionate and purposeful businesses.

2. **Set clear boundaries between work and home** Avoid talking shop all of the time outside work. While you may have some of your best ideas chatting at the dinner table, try to draw the line. Consider creating some rules to set those boundaries, such as no 'talking shop' at weekends.

3. **Make business a priority** In running a family business, focus on making the business viable and profitable, rather than overemphasising the importance of the family to the business. Cherry-pick the positive traits of family values and unity, but focus on building the business as a priority. The family will benefit in the long run.

4. **Align expectations across generations to avoid conflict** Figure out precisely what each family member wants from the business. Some might see it merely as a source of income and a financial asset; others will see it as providing career opportunities for the family or as a means for contributing to the community. Some may see its heritage as a legacy to be passed on from generation to generation; others may have shorter-term expectations and ambitions. Whatever the case, it is vital to know each individual's expectations, understand and appreciate the differences between them and be clear

about which expectations are likely to be met. That way, the expectations of the family and the overall vision for the firm can be aligned and supported.

5. **Nurture individuality and respect differences**   While there tends to be unity in family businesses – and this can be a great strength – it is also important to respect differences between individuals and foster independence. Each person's creativity, ambitions, ideas and skills should be understood, valued and nurtured. Differences should be celebrated because diverse teams with different yet complementary experiences and viewpoints, are generally the most successful. When individuality is nurtured within a united family team, that team is greatly empowered to achieve its goals and those of the individuals within it.

In order to maximise the potential of a family business, owners and their teams need to address each of the challenges discussed above while also harnessing the power of their unique competitive advantages. As they do so, they must have clear processes, firm rules and absolute accountability to ensure that the business will succeed across the generations.

Chapter 2

Conflict and Compromise

Introduction

Conflict and compromise are inevitable in all businesses. Differences of opinion will arise, problems will crop up that challenge the owners and staff, and personality clashes are common. Nonetheless, businesses keep going, which is a testament to the other side of the coin: compromise. For every problem in business, there is a solution, and it often involves meeting halfway on an issue or an opinion. In a family business, however, this can be a more delicate balancing act because of the relationships at the heart of the business. It is often an inescapable fact that emotions and emotion-driven agendas can infect the business. Sometimes this can be a conscious act – such as gaining petty revenge within the business for something that occurred within the family, or vice versa; sometimes it can be unconscious, stemming from the roles embedded in the family over time that can influence family members' behaviour. Managing conflict and compromise in the context of a family business, therefore, requires tact, sensitivity and well-marked boundaries for interaction and behaviour.

"Never assume anything," advises TV presenter and hotelier Alex Polizzi, based on her experience of working in a family business:

> "The more honesty there is, and the more formalised the structure is, the easier things are. I just think that honesty and facing up to why things are as they are is the most important thing; not brushing anything under the table. That's important."[1]

Conflict can have many sources, such as unsound assumptions, disparate expectations or a lack of honesty or transparency, but most of these can be resolved by clear and honest communication around what every member thinks and expects regarding the business and

---

[1] Polizzi, A. Interview with author (June/July 2013).

their place in it. To create a successful business, family members must be able to effectively work together as a team. If there is constant arguing, with the same issues resurfacing time and time again and barely suppressed emotions bubbling under the surface, this will drain the business of the energy, drive and passion it needs to survive, let alone thrive.

Whether conflict is an occasional problem or is ongoing at a low level, family members must be able to effectively identify solutions and implement them. In this chapter, I will examine two of the most common and most divisive areas of conflict in family businesses: sibling rivalry and parent–child relationships. Alongside this, I will examine the ways families can deal with such problems through well-planned, intelligent compromise.

Conflict: Family vs. Business

A family business is made up of two distinct systems that can prove to be incompatible. On the one hand there is the business, where the best talent is selected on the basis of competence, relationships are essentially contractual and limited, decisions are rational and logical and profits are the ultimate goal. On the other hand, there is the family, where everyone is included in the team on the basis of belonging, rather than competence. In a family, decisions can often be based on emotion rather than reason. Whereas money is the key driving force of the business, love is the currency and engine of the family unit. It's not surprising, then, that there is such scope for conflict when those systems collide.

Issues that Cause Conflict in a Family Business

The most common causes of conflict in family businesses are as follows:

- Confusion over what is expected of individuals in terms of their roles, level of effort and time, responsibilities, remuneration, rewards and boundaries as a result of false, unconfirmed assumptions and expectations.

- Feeling undervalued and disrespected due to a lack of empathy or understanding for each other's skills, abilities and feelings.
- A culture of entitlement, which leads to dissatisfaction and disappointment for those who are under the impression that they have an automatic right to a career in the family business, and also to demotivation among non-family members if the younger generation is given preferential treatment simply for being family.
- The role and rights of in-laws and whether they are welcomed or excluded from being involved in the business.
- Lack of fairness, where someone else seems to be getting preferential treatment.
- Sibling rivalry and competitiveness.
- Parent–child relationship issues (most commonly between father and son) regarding control, power and the psychological and professional complexities around proving oneself on the one hand, and letting go on the other.

While all of these potential sources of conflict are important to be aware of and prepare for, in my experience it is the last two – sibling rivalry and parent–child relationships (particularly those between fathers and sons) – that tend to be the primary causes of conflict in family businesses.

Father–Son Relationships

In family businesses, conflict often arises between the founder and the potential successor. In other words, typically the father business-owner and his son, the inheritor. As a unique emotional entity, the parent–child relationship has been the subject of extensive psychological study, and it is clear that those background psychological and emotional factors can play a role in business, too. A lot can depend on how the father views the business. If, in his mind, it is an extension of himself, a manifestation of his work ethic, professionalism and power, then it is likely he will view his son, his successor, with some level of resentment. This can manifest itself in many ways, but however it arises, it will be detrimental to the structure and operations of the business. It can also be further complicated by emotional reactions to aging and letting go, which can intensify the mixed feelings he has towards his son. For his part, the son is perhaps overly anxious to prove himself and his worth as a successor, unwittingly inviting his father's anger even as he strives to do everything perfectly. Inevitably, the son ends up believing that his father doesn't trust him, doesn't rate him as a professional, and things can very quickly turn sour from there. Add in the conflict between 'how it's always been done' and the younger generation's drive to modernise, and there is a volcano of conflict just waiting to erupt.

The two men's difference of approach infiltrates all aspects of their relationship, from remuneration to working hours to ownership of shares and attitudes to staff. The father's 'old retainers', who have grown up in the business with him and have great loyalty to him, may well be reluctant to take direction from the son and may even check with the father before carrying out the son's instructions. The younger members of staff might be quicker to recognise and accept the son's approach, creating two camps at war with one another. The father's perception of the son's ingratitude, lack of appreciation and loyalty is matched by the son's demand for a reasonable degree of independence in his approach to the business.

The effect of such internecine conflict is an undermining of the business's focus, detracting from the productivity and well-being of the workforce. Therefore, there is a great need to devise strategies that will enable this key relationship to develop in a way that is not destructive to the business or the family.

Handling Father–Son Conflict

Father–son relations in a family business setting can be stressful because the expectations of the father are pitted against the expectations of the son, often culminating in an inability to communicate these to each other effectively. The emotional factors further muddy the waters: the son wants his father to be proud of him; the father wants to guide his son in the right way. Although it may seem intractable while in the thick of it, this issue can be addressed and resolved. The following measures can greatly reduce the potential for father–son conflict:

- From a relatively young age, invite the son to work in the family business during school holidays to give him a feel for the business and a solid grounding in its operations.
- Start the conversation about the succession of the family business by assuring the son that should he wish to join the business, he

will be welcomed and supported, but that if he wishes to pursue another career path, he will receive the same level of support and encouragement.

- Outline expectations in terms of what, if any, role the son might have in the future; that it is not a given that he will immediately take over the running of the business, that he will have to prove himself and that he has the capacity to do so. For example, advise the son that he must fulfil certain entry criteria before applying for a position in the business. Entry criteria might include third-level education plus a number of years working outside the family business.

Once the son has gained the relevant experience and decided he wants to pursue a career in the family business, it is essential that he and his father map out and cultivate a healthy working relationship. Useful steps in achieving this sort of working relationship are set out below:

- Create a welcoming atmosphere, which would involve the father being approachable so that the son can come to him with any questions, issues or concerns. Sometimes fathers can be so pre-occupied with preventing accusations of nepotism that they treat their sons with less evident respect or care than other members of staff.

- Sit down and work out what each person's respective responsibilities and duties are and how they might change or evolve over time. It's important that this arrangement is documented, so that it can be consulted should issues arise.

- Create a distinct division of the business over which the son has managerial autonomy. Developing this division will allow the son to exercise and improve his managerial skills, thereby gaining the respect and trust of fellow employees as well as his father.

- If the father–son relationship becomes contentious, hire an outside facilitator to meet with both parties and ascertain the nature of the difficulties they are experiencing. He or she would then meet with each party separately to ensure that party A understands party B's position, and vice versa. All the issues will be teased out and a plan drawn up that will meet the requirements of both parties. Though this may require some organisational and/or structural changes in the business, it should enable each to have a better understanding of the other's position and help them to work in a more harmonious way.

- It is important to talk about feelings around succession openly and as early as possible. For the father, succession is a very sensitive issue, involving fears about his future financial security, his standing and prestige with his employees, customers, suppliers and in the community. While the responsibility for introducing the son to the business lies initially with the father, the responsibility for dealing with the succession should be shared by both father and son. If they have developed a good working relationship over time, they are more likely to realise the potential for stress and to work to relieve this. Father and son should work out a plan for the succession process to take place at a pace that suits them both. The family, the management team and staff should be informed of the plan. (See **Chapter 10** for more detailed discussion on succession.)

Sibling Rivalry

When a family has an established business, there is a strong possibility that one or more of the children will become interested in joining, or be encouraged by their parents to join, the family enterprise. Too often, however, parents unconsciously sow the seeds of future sibling rivalry when they promote a competitive spirit among their children in the belief that they are helping their development, but the end result may not be what they hoped for. In other situations parents are so anxious to ensure that all the children are treated equally that they give them equal shares in the business; but this approach has many drawbacks, and business owners should give careful consideration to the outcome of such decisions.

It is vital to discuss each sibling's expectations and, for the good of the business, ask them to carefully and honestly consider who is the most suitable successor in terms of skills, experience and leadership ability. It may not necessarily be the eldest sibling. Indeed, as we shall see in the case study about the Zegna family in **Chapter 7**, the youngest child may in fact be the next natural leader for the firm.

The handling of the children's roles within the business is an essential component in ensuring a successful transition to the next generation. The traditional principle of *primogenitor* held that the eldest male heir should inherit all of his father's estate. Though cultural adherence to this principle has become greatly diluted over time, there are nevertheless many families who are still influenced by it when it comes to choosing a successor for their business. Indeed, one potential successor once told me that while he did not expect to inherit all of the family business, as the eldest male heir he ought to get the 'lion's share' of the business; not because he worked harder or more effectively than his brother and sisters, but purely because he was the *eldest male heir*. Evidently, expectations around rights, roles and succession should be discussed early on to prevent misconceptions or incorrect assumptions that could ultimately undermine both the business and family relations.

What follows is an example that illustrates the potential outcomes of sibling rivalry. In the case study below about M I Dickson, we see how rivalry and misunderstandings threaten the family business, and how tackling the issues head-on leads to their resolution.

CASE STUDY: M I DICKSON LTD – MISMATCHED SIBLING ASPIRATIONS

The family pork butcher business M I Dickson was first introduced in **Chapter 1** and provides an interesting example of a successful business now being run by the second generation. In managing the business, brother and sister partners Michael and Christine Dickson overcame many obstacles and never had any major disagreements, despite working together from their teenage years until Christine sadly passed away in June 2013 at the age of 62. Sometimes their opinions differed significantly and they needed a serious discussion of the issues involved, but they always worked things out. They witnessed how things could go wrong when family members didn't address issues in another family business, and were determined not to let their personal lives or business be adversely affected by their familial difficulties. In an interview with the author,[2] Michael Dickson described how he and his sister managed sibling relations in order to forge a solid business model:

---

[2] Dickson, M. Interview with author (July 2013). M I Dickson Ltd of South Tyneside, England, is referred to throughout this book as an excellent example of a family business and it is discussed in more detail in **Chapter 6**.

"When my dad first went into partnership with a friend after the war, it seems to have been unequal in effort and contribution and lasted no more than five years; my father obviously believed he could reap greater rewards by going it alone. I think it's inevitable that most close relationships with friends and family change once you marry or have a partner and children. That split was just a symptom of new priorities emerging as they do in all close relationships as we go through life. Had he not followed his dream, I think the perceived lack of fulfilment would probably have turned into unhealthy and destructive frustration.

"I think it's fair to say that Chris didn't have the same level of drive and ambition as I did. She had no dependents, of course, which is a game changer, and while she liked the idea of growth, she wasn't naturally disposed to defining the necessary pathways and tackling whatever constraints lay in our way. That was more my forte.

"I was a bit madder, couldn't take no for an answer, more the workaholic who worried away at problems until I found the solution. To paraphrase the words of Bill Shankly, the business to me wasn't a matter of life and death, it was much more important than that."

It can be quite common for one sibling or partner to feel that they are putting in more effort than the other. This only becomes a problem if it is not openly discussed and a win–win solution uncovered.

"It came to a head when we had outgrown our first factory. I was increasingly conscious of how much I was driving growth and while Chris's calm, administrative and organisational skills were pivotal in maintaining close control and profitability, I always felt the pure entrepreneurial spirit was mine."

Fortunately, Michael had a sounding board in the form of the then managing partner of their accountants, who knew both personalities intimately.

"You need that dependable, fair-minded *other* whom you trust implicitly, someone who will listen impartially and help you to a conclusion but not necessarily hand you the answer."

Ultimately, they agreed that the best course of action would be for Michael to address his concerns with Christine because their relationship was coming under increasing pressure. To avoid resentment growing and damaging their relationship irretrievably, Michael gathered his courage and spoke with his sister

"I loved and respected her deeply, but knew I had to be fairly direct, so I said something like, 'We've always been great partners and our complementary skills have taken us forward, but I've been considering going on my own as I don't think the current drawings and shareholding truly reflect my efforts in growing the company.'

"She said, 'Draw more than me, if that's what you need,' but that wasn't what I wanted. I needed something more formal, and clear recognition. I said, 'We're both directors, but I'm looking for the MD title and a majority shareholding.' That was agreed without further drama, but while I'm sure that it hurt and offended her, I could see no other way of keeping us together long term and, in her heart, I believe she knew that.

"I can't have any regrets because that move guaranteed we would continue to work together. Relations eventually thawed and I went on to deliver an ongoing programme of expansion which saw us both better off. That ultimately had to be better than allowing stagnation or an unbridgeable rift to develop."

The fact is that siblings in a family business will be different. Some will avoid confronting issues, preferring to ignore them; others will address them and voice concerns and work to find a solution. Some prioritise work over everything else; others prioritise lifestyle and family. The critical point is that such differences should be acknowledged, discussed and accepted. Nobody is necessarily right or wrong; different opinions and ways of working should be accepted and a compromise reached to ensure that everyone is happy.

Michael says that Christine would probably have continued to ignore the developing tension rather than confront it head-on.

"That was indicative of who Chris was," says Michael. "She would have happily continued to walk around the rock in the middle of the floor where I just couldn't, and that was probably the difference between us. As I said earlier, we brought complementary skills to the business. Chris was deeply respected and while I continued to deliver the growth and arguably the vision, she kept us tight administratively and maintained a steely grip on the financials."

One of the things that drove this need to resolve the issue was having seen his wife's family business marred by a lack of communication. As Michael explains: "When we were married, my wife's family had a much bigger and longer-established family business than we did: an Italian ice cream business with several parlours, vans, fish and chip shops and various other enterprises. Marisa's grandfather set it up in the 1920s, and while there were six siblings, it was probably my father-in-law, the eldest, who proved to be the one to carry forward and develop the business. When his father died, he appeared to be the steady producer and ideas man, moving the business on for the family at large; but it seems their relationships changed fairly quickly, without the patriarchal figurehead.

"I realised he wasn't speaking to his brothers, and relations with his sisters seemed to show some tension and that it seemed to stem from their differing outlooks on life. The business fragmented in what seems to have been a fairly informal manner which left them partly connected. It always seemed to me that it would have been much better had it been kept together and developed as a whole with a clear management structure, or formally divided so each could get on with their own lives. There was a wealth of family talent and I'm sure a proud name would have endured and family wealth been maintained along with valuable employment, if structured arrangements had been made for whichever route they chose to follow.

"They were previously a very close group I believe, but tended to avoid talking over money issues out of love and respect for each other. Perhaps that mutual lack of candour fed their divisions and actually precipitated a breakdown in relationships which saw my father-in-law and his brothers barely speaking for 20 years. When the last site closed down, largely through inertia and growing despair at the situation, I remember my father-in-law describing it as being like a death in the family, and in a way it was."

Sadly, this kind of story is not a rare one and yet it would simply not occur in a non-family business. As can happen, the family system got in the way of the business system – and one destroyed the other.

How to Work Harmoniously as Siblings

Misunderstandings are more likely to arise where siblings fail to realise or accept that their interactions with each other are driven by psychological factors, one of which is rivalry. It is important to ensure that systems are developed to keep rivalry to a minimum. If the family business is large enough, rivalry can be minimised by siblings taking responsibility for separate areas, defined operationally or geographically. In my experience, it is far better to openly discuss the potential for sibling rivalry and conflict so that family members can have their say and then participate in planning an operating policy that will quell arguments quickly and solve disagreements effectively. Such a policy could include actions such as:

- clearly defining the role and job title of each sibling in the business along with expectations around the level of effort/time expected of them;
- adopting fair and sensible policies dealing with matters such as remuneration, performance appraisal, promotion and even dismissal;
- outlining expectations and ambitions for the firm early on and understanding that priorities may change over time; and

- establishing a clear understanding that when differences arise between siblings, they should sit down and discuss the issues in a calm atmosphere and endeavour to resolve the problem themselves before seeking outside assistance.

While rivalry is commonplace in family businesses and need not be worried about unduly, it is best to face it head-on and resolve it for the sake of the business rather than letting it turn into a bigger argument. Family members may need reminding that if they look after the business, the business will look after them. With this in mind, having independent directors can add huge value in the area of sibling conflict because they can help bring objectivity to the situation.

General Points on Conflict Prevention and Management

Well-adjusted families realise that conflict can and will occur, and they seek advice on how to confront and manage it. These families have usually learned hard lessons from past experience, and they all tend to share the following characteristics:

- **Commitment to and prioritising of family unity**   While family members are free to pursue their own goals, they will not engage in any activity that threatens the interests of the family.
- **Mutual appreciation and communication**   Appreciation and awareness of the strengths and weaknesses of family members, playing to their strengths and affording adequate personal space to each member. Communicating openly, honestly and frequently.
- **Spending time together**   Strong families enjoy each other's company, not just in the business but also in leisure activities, while at the same time not crowding each other out.
- **Strong values**   Values such as integrity, honesty and a strong commitment to one's beliefs are essential.
- **Ability to cope with crisis and stress**   Learning to cope with stress and deal with crises are normal parts of life, but some of us do it more successfully than others. Strong families keep crises in perspective while looking for positive approaches to resolve them.[3] They do not brush things under the carpet, are not secretive and are not afraid to look for outside help.

[3]   Stinnett, N. and DeFrain, J., *Secrets of Strong Families* (Little, Brown, 1986).

All family businesses can learn from these characteristics of successful families in business. It is clear that it is not only the business that requires constant and innovative investment of time and energy – the family unit itself, and all of the relationships within it, also requires constant investment of time and energy. This is to ensure that issues are dealt with quickly and effectively, that family members feel heard and valued and that the whole enterprise feels like a natural and enjoyable extension of family life, where each member is encouraged, supported and valued for their unique contribution. It's not easy to achieve this, but it is very possible. It is important to remember that conflict is normal and differences of opinion are healthy.

The following is a list of tips to help **prevent** the most common types of conflict experienced in family businesses. They may appear to be simple, common-sense guidelines, but in my experience they are, in fact, rarely applied.

Tips for Preventing Conflict

1. Consider the types of issue that could arise and put relevant mechanisms in place to prevent them. For example, is it easy for all employees, both family and non-family, to contribute their views? Are those views listened to, valued and considered? If so, you will avoid the problem of employees feeling undervalued or ignored. If not, then you are quite simply asking for trouble.

2. Regularly remind each other of the family's values, goals and vision to build mutual trust, respect and harmony, reinforce commitment and maximise understanding of the priorities, purpose and direction of the business. This could be incorporated into every family meeting (or quarterly meetings at least).

3. Communicate and collaborate openly, honestly and often in order to resolve issues before they have a chance to escalate.

4. Replace informal father–son/father–daughter interactions with professional chairman/CEO–managing director meetings, as

in non-family businesses. Avoid informal conversations that could lead to spontaneous conflict; establish instead structured, regular (weekly) meetings with agendas in order to place relationships in a controlled, non-emotional environment conducive to productive discussion and problem solving.

5. Depersonalise processes that could ordinarily be marred by emotion by putting in place an agreed family policy on 'what we will do when such-and-such a conflict arises'. Consider the types of issue that can arise and discuss and record what processes will be used to deal with them if they do. In a family charter or constitution (see **Chapter 6**), agree clear and specific rules about how decisions will be made and disputes resolved. A family charter or constitution is a document that sets out the values, philosophies, rules and expectations of family members involved in the business. It is a living document that requires frequent revision to meet the needs of the family and the business. It is really a summary of policies about how the family and business interact. It will also include the family's vision and mission statement. The document is for family members only.

Where, despite best intentions, conflict does arise, there are a number of ways to **resolve** the problem and stop it from escalating further.

TIPS FOR CONFLICT RESOLUTION

1. Address problems quickly rather than letting them fester.

2. Refer to the family charter or constitution (see **Chapter 6**) to understand the consensus view about what to do when an issue arises and follow that process accordingly.

3. Hold a family meeting to resolve issues by talking them through calmly, with or without an external facilitator.

4. Try to empathise with the other person, stepping into their shoes to see things from their point of view.

5. During discussions with family members, use 'I' or 'me' rather than 'you' to avoid falling into the vicious circle of perceived blame and subsequent defensiveness. For example, instead of saying, "you are always interrupting me and you never listen", say, "it makes me feel annoyed and not valued when people interrupt me". Choose your words carefully to keep the conversation away from emotional pitfalls.

6. Identify the issue and outline the position/opinion/feelings of each party involved. Consider the ideal outcome for each party and draw up a list of potential win–win options. Discuss and select the best one, reflect on it, and then monitor its implementation.

7. Devise and implement mediating structures, such as a family forum, to develop win–win solutions. Have a family rule about the importance of compromise. Seek out the common ground and focus on that. For instance, in Japan the term 'saving face' is used for the act of discussing issues for as long as it takes to arrive at a win–win solution, i.e. where neither party loses face. This requires the ability to compromise and share power, so that all parties see a benefit in the final outcome. Everyone should feel like they have 'won' in some way, even if they've had to compromise. So look at potential solutions that serve the interests of everybody involved. Explore possibilities, reframe the issue, wonder about potential solutions and scenarios, and discuss until you find the situation.

8. View conflict as being a potential driver for change. After all, without conflict different perspectives might be lost and the business could suffer. Conflicts create a certain dynamic to the business and encourage family members to reconsider and evaluate strategic plans – and that is often a good thing.

9. Bring in an external mediator, arbitrator or facilitator where necessary. An impartial, professional person can be invaluable in these circumstances. While family businesses tend to prefer to keep their disputes private, and the introduction of

a mediator therefore may not appeal, they can be the best option as they will be impartial and discreet. Sometimes external advisors are necessary when there is too much history and entrenched polarity for family members to be able to see, and discuss, the situation clearly.

10. Once the conflict has been resolved, prevent it from happening again by discussing it fully, looking for patterns and triggers, identifying risk areas and how to handle them. Hold follow-up meetings to ensure the issues have been truly resolved to everyone's satisfaction.

In the first part of this book, we have examined the particular advantages and challenges of being a family business, which largely stem from the overlap between the personal and professional. The family business is a unique model and, as we have seen, it requires deft handling and constant evaluation to keep both the personal and the professional running steadily and smoothly. We have also looked at the general make-up and structure of the family business and identified the areas where conflict can arise and how such issues can be addressed and resolved.

Part II is wide-reaching in scope, covering a number of key factors and concerns. It examines the governance of a family business, how to free the business from the inhibiting aspects of family involvement and how to professionalise the business by bringing in independent advisors and non-family board members. It is an overview of the ways and means to create, maintain and pass on a viable, efficient, cost-effective business that can be improved, expanded and grown through the generations.

Part II

The Family and the Business

CHAPTER 3

Communication and Culture, Vision and Stewardship

Introduction

As **Chapters 1** and **2** have shown, the family business is a unique model with its own challenges and opportunities. Interlinking a family system with a business system creates a specific set of factors that must be understood fully by all concerned if progress is to be made. At its base, the family business is built on four cornerstones:

1. Good communication across all interrelationships
2. A strong, values-led culture
3. A clear, well-described vision
4. Careful and conscientious stewardship of the entire enterprise

Once all of these elements are present and protected, the business will be able to move into the future with confidence; if any of these elements is missing, this will seriously undermine the stability of the business and can lead to failure. It is therefore essential to consider these four cornerstones with great care – they are the foundation of the family enterprise.

1. Communication

There seems to be a disconnect between what a family thinks about its business and how it actually operates that business. Studies have found that while family business respondents cite issues around relationships and communication as the main challenge they face, a staggering 86% do not have rules or policies in place for dealing with predictable family business issues or expectation/relationship management, nor do they hold regular family meetings to share information and achieve consensus. Furthermore, very few have conflict-management processes in place, such as family councils or charters (see **Chapter 6**), to achieve equilibrium between business and family or establish consensus.

So, it appears that while family business owners know that communication is a crucial issue, the majority do not act on this knowledge in order to resolve their issues. This is quite hard to understand, and it undoubtedly contributes heavily to the reasons behind the fact that only around one-third of businesses survive to the second generation, with as few as 10% making it to the third generation (see **Chapter 1**).

Communication within the Family

When family members are also co-workers, it is essential that they prioritise open and honest communication with one another. A business is as strong as its connections, so if weaknesses are allowed to take root (for example in the form of taboo subjects or repressing opinions or not sharing information), this can infect and destabilise the whole business system. It can be difficult, of course, to broach sensitive issues such as succession, spousal rights and inheritance issues, but it is nonetheless imperative that the family puts in place ways and means of having these discussions in a constructive and useful manner. This means ensuring inclusiveness – that all family members feel their opinions and contributions have been heard. It also means stressing the importance of consensus, so that individuals don't feel resentful if their particular idea does not become the action taken. It is a matter of managing relationships and people carefully and respectfully, with a defined awareness of where the flashpoints and contentious issues lie, so that they can be navigated with due care and consideration.

Promoting and ensuring good communication among family members delivers many benefits, such as:

- eliminating assumptions around what other people's expectations/feelings/needs are;
- enabling open discussions that result in honesty, transparency and accountability and mutual trust and respect, which in turn creates strong long-term relationships;
- bringing clarity and consensus around vision, objectives and control;
- replacing resentment, exclusion and confusion with commitment, inclusion and motivation; and
- being able to express oneself in a creative environment allows for innovation, creativity and fulfilment of potential.

By contrast, the consequences of poor relationships and inadequate communication include:

- missed opportunities and lost productivity due to arguing;
- focusing conversations on family issues instead of business matters;
- ignoring each other, talking behind each other's backs; and
- refusing to talk about key issues.

It is essential that every family member is taught from the outset how much is at stake in family relationship issues. Every member must understand that these issues, if not handled correctly, can have a massive impact on the business and create a negative, counterproductive atmosphere.

The starting point for good communication is to open the necessary channels and establish the forums that provide the framework within which communication will take place. In this way, the business is prioritised above personal issues and family members are forced to consider their viewpoints within that logical, fair framework and address their issues accordingly. It essentially creates a safe haven for discussion, regardless of how difficult the matter at hand is.

It needs to be a stated philosophy of the business that disagreements can be healthy and drivers of creativity and positive change; that they should not be feared or avoided. As long as there are measures in place to prevent and resolve major conflicts, then lively discussions and heated debates should not be discouraged; they can be left at the office door when the family goes home. The means of establishing this sort of framework is set out in detail in **Chapter 6**, which sets out the role and function of family councils and constitutions.

How to Communicate Effectively with Each Other

- Consider body language: 70% of all communication is non-verbal, so honesty is all the more important (your body language can call your honesty into question).

- Be aware of your tone of voice and avoid superiority, sarcasm, anger or self-doubt.

- Practise active listening: pay attention and show interest in what others say and you'll be shown the same courtesy. Be constructive in your responses.

- Repeat back and summarise what you have been told, for example: "So, if I understand you correctly, you are saying…" This ensures that key messages are being accurately understood.

- Listen properly: when someone is talking and we are supposed to be listening, a number of things can happen – we might get distracted, wandering off from what they're saying to what we're thinking. Noises or activities in our environment may momentarily distract us. If we are not engaged or interested in what someone is saying or we are stressed with too much to do, we may only partially listen and focus on our own priorities. Hearing only part of a message is detrimental, in that we will have a deficient and distorted understanding of what has been said. So it is important to focus on listening and understanding what is being said and minimise interruption in order to avoid misunderstandings and arguments.

- Practise empathy: try to care about the other person and their concerns, opinions and perspective. Have a positive attitude about people and never disregard someone else's feelings or opinions.

- Agree to disagree, if necessary.

- Spend sufficient time with family members out of the office and agree not to 'talk shop' during these times. Get to know each other and deepen existing bonds on a personal level. This helps to build up a reserve of humour, goodwill and understanding to draw upon during less harmonious times. When you know someone well on a personal level, you may be more inclined to give them the benefit of the doubt and see the whole story when necessary.

- Meet regularly in a professional capacity, too, to discuss issues, resolve problems, air concerns and agree a way forward. Focus on business issues rather than personal problems at these times, which can be dealt with at home/outside the working environment.

- Enable constructive feedback by putting in place mechanisms for all stakeholders to share their views (family and non-family). Encourage everyone to participate and feel included.

- Organise team-building 'away days' to discuss vision, strategy, problems and solutions, as well as holding communication exercises in which participants may share personal events that have affected them, explain the way they behave/communicate and discuss the main challenges they face at work and in the business. Split time between these business-focused discussions and play/social activities. Encourage interaction between different affinity groups by bringing them together to form new relationships. Ask each participant what they hope to get out of the sessions (for themselves, the business and the family) and to voice any concerns they may have.

- Appoint external advisors and facilitators when necessary so that emotions don't get in the way of clarity around business issues. Such advisors could facilitate discussions that may be fractious.

- See **Chapter 2**, 'Conflict and Compromise', for more tips on how to 'run' a successful family within a successful business.

Communicating Effectively with the Board

While the composition, role and responsibilities of the board of directors are examined in **Chapter 6**, here we are concerned with the communication channels between the family and the board. The basic prerequisite for communication at this level is an understanding on all sides regarding the respective roles and responsibilities of the family owners/shareholders, board members and the executive managers of the business. Each strand of the business has its own remit and it is vital that each understands the remit of the others. In this way, there is clarity surrounding the discussion and resolution of issues, how action will be taken and who will implement it. In essence, then:

- the shareholders/family/owners make strategic policy decisions, decisions around profitability and liquidity, set goals around growth and define the vision and values that underpin the business; and
- the shareholders/family/owners are represented by the board, whose members must plot the course of the business in the medium to long term. The main tasks of the board are to:

  1. approve and monitor the company's performance;
  2. protect and represent the interests of the shareholders as a whole; and
  3. provide entrepreneurial leadership of the company within a framework of prudent controls which enables risk to be assessed and managed. (*The Combined Code* 2003)

The executive managers/senior management (sometimes referred to as the 'management team') is generally a team of individuals at the highest level of organisational management who have the day-to-day responsibilities of managing a company or corporation. They hold specific executive powers conferred onto them by the board of directors and/or the shareholders. The executive management typically consists of the heads of the firm's product and/or geographic units and of functional executives such as the chief financial officer or the chief operating officer.

Dr Ivan Lansberg defines the difference between owners (shareholders) and managers as follows:

"Imagine the family business is a Boeing 737. Owners have a right to choose what the plane is used for – for example, passengers or cargo – and they might decide on different risk profiles (like whether to heap up debt in order to expand the fleet). But owners stay out of the cockpit, they do not serve drinks or collect garbage.

They let the pilot and the crew do their jobs. The trouble is, inherited shares don't come with a user manual, and one of the toughest challenges families in business face is in educating their members about ownership, and defining their rights, roles and responsibilities."[1]

It may be a tough challenge, but once these interlinking roles have been set out clearly and agreed, communication will be smooth and effective between all parties. The way to achieve this is through a family charter or constitution (see **Chapter 6**), which describes the functions of each part of the business, how each part relates to the others and how the channels of communication should operate between them. This effectively provides a template for effective communication, allowing the family to communicate with the board as one voice, delivering agreed decisions and views to the board, thus saving time and pointless argument. These systems are essential to the smooth operation of the business.

How to Facilitate Good Communication between the Family and the Board

- Ensure everyone is clear (having read the documented rules) about which decisions are specifically reserved for shareholders and which are delegated to the board.

- Ensure that there is a rule about what to do for borderline cases that are tipping towards shareholder final decision. For example, the shareholding family members may examine those cases on their own merits and decide whether the board or family should have the final say.

---

[1] Lansberg, I., "Governance Structure for a Complex Family Enterprise", paper delivered at IFB Master Class 6: Professionalising Governance in the Family Firm, London, 29 September 2005.

EXAMPLE: DELEGATION – STRUTT AND PARKER (FARMS) LTD.

Fifth-generation family business Strutt and Parker, which manages 20,000 acres of farmland in Suffolk and Essex, did this in 2012, when there were local protests about company proposals to erect wind farms near a village. The shareholder group did not wish to divide communities, so they weighed up all the issues and decided that it should be a matter for the board, rather than a policy decision for the owners. The board subsequently examined the facts and decided on which side of the line the issue fell.[2]

- Clarify how the board and the family should interact (i.e. through which representative and/or method).

- Put all important communications in writing.

- Have a family member sit on the board either as chairman or in a non-participatory role to ensure that the family is adequately represented and the family charter is respected.

- Hold joint meetings from time to time where the family council and board sit together to discuss matters.

- Enable further two-way interaction by inviting the MD/CEO to family council meetings and having the chairperson of the family council attend occasional board meetings.

- Regularly measure the board's performance and the family's satisfaction with the board (see **Chapter 5**).

---

[2] Institute for Family Business, "Case Study: Strutt & Parker (Farms)", www.ifb.org.uk.

CASE STUDY: M I DICKSON LTD –
COMMUNICATING EFFECTIVELY WITH THE BOARD[3]

Michael Dickson, MD of M I Dickson Ltd, who ran the business with his sister, found the establishment of a family council greatly improved communication from everyone's perspective.

"I suppose Chris and I acted like overbearing parents, and while we appointed lots of people with titles we still tended to oversee and interfere in all areas of operations, which isn't conducive to the development of good managers. Saying, 'Don't do that, I'll do it myself and I'll be quicker' is a classic case of small-business thinking and ineffective management.

"Once we started thinking seriously about how we were preparing for retirement and developing the existing team, things began to change. We did the unthinkable: we actually started to hold regular meetings. Historically, Christine and I would take strategic and operational decisions, but the management team was never party to how we arrived at those decisions. We accepted we had to change that approach and become far more transparent and inclusive if we were going to see our management team fully engaged and contributing.

"The past five years or so have seen a sea change in how we communicate at all levels in the business and how decisions are reached. That change was more or less concurrent with the creation of our family council. We've undoubtedly moved forward and it sometimes feels we have a meeting overload. The family council receives a monthly financial update and reports from the monthly senior management meetings. The family council chair attends quarterly board meetings and we come together for twice-yearly formal family council meetings. It's now a family event that sees everyone coming home and we make a point of enjoying family meals together and generally having a good time. It's brought us even closer.

---

[3] Dickson, M. Interview with author (July 2013).

"My family (the next generation) speak to me far more bluntly about business matters than they would have previously, because they wouldn't have wanted to seem presumptuous or offend, which can scupper clear communication. It's not that they were in any sense unable to speak their mind, but our family board gives them a forum to air their views freely, so you have an opportunity to hear what ambitions they hold personally and for their family business."

2. A Culture Built on Common Values

Values are essentially the human side of a business: they bind the family, define the culture and enrich the business. As the core principles shaping the way business is done, they sum up precisely what makes a business special and what it stands for. A business's core value might be to stand behind the quality of the product, and any product not reaching the satisfactory standard is automatically eliminated. Core values are timeless and do not change; they are sustainable in the long term. Examples of such values include:

- **Accountability:** acknowledging and taking responsibility for actions, products, decision and policies. This can be applied to the individual and to the company.
- **Community:** contributing to society and demonstrating corporate social responsibility.
- **Integrity:** acting with honesty and without compromising the truth.

The starting point in determining common values in a family business is to seek and secure agreement on which principles the family applies in the business and the culture within it. What values are important to each person? By posing this question to each family member, you will uncover the values you hold in common and be able to determine which are the most important.

It is likely that if the business has a long heritage and a tradition, common values have already been established. But are these still valid for the business today? Below are some exercises and questionnaires designed to help a family business identify the most relevant and important values shared by all family members. Armed with this information, it will then be possible to draft a section on values in the family charter or constitution (see **Chapter 6**). These core principles will become part of the daily working life of the business and be a guide to future generations and employees.

The values of the business should inform everything, from how staff answer the phone to how the company is branded in the marketplace. After all, the role of the core values is to inform vision, culture, purpose, mission, strategy, brand identity, policies and standards. From those values the mission statement of the business is created (see 'A Shared Vision' later in this chapter), which is then translated into deliverable actions, policies and principles.

Values and purpose are the foundation of the business and join each area together, from recruiting a dream team of talented people who will go the extra mile for your business to strategic planning, raising finance and, crucially, succession to the next generation. The value set should be embedded into the very heart of the enterprise so that it engages every single stakeholder, from customers and staff to partners and suppliers.

Benefits of Knowing the Core Values of the Business

Many of the benefits of defining your core values are intangible, but they are nevertheless very important. While the profit margin won't suddenly shoot up because a document has been drafted stating the values by which the business operates, the effect of stating the values should be felt in other ways, for example:

1. **Family unity** Shared values and traditions bind the family and the business together, maintaining and strengthening those bonds, particularly as the family grows apart geographically and generationally. The stated values act as a reminder of who the family is and what their business aims to achieve.
2. **Strength of vision** A business that is based on core values, with an ethical heart at its centre, offers a better vision of its future to staff and shareholders alike. It makes people feel that they are part of something larger than just 'bean-counting'; that they are an important part of the business, not just a number on a payslip. This intangible sense of pride and belonging is an important side effect of stating the agreed values of the business.

3. **Resilience** Values-led businesses are often tougher and more focused in the face of adversity, which creates a virtuous circle. There is more to fall back on than simply product units and KPIs – there is an underlying bond that ensures everyone works hard to keep the business going in difficult times.

4. **Customer loyalty** Once values are communicated to customers, it can have a positive impact on customer loyalty. If a customer admires and relates to the stated core values of a business, he or she will feel part of that greater whole and enjoy doing business in this way.

5. **Brand perception** Branding isn't merely what a business looks like, it's about what it is and how it conducts itself. A business's values speak to the hearts as well as the minds of customers. This can be used to add value and distinctiveness to the company's public profile (see the Zegna case study below). Brands with longevity are purposeful and have strong values that win people's loyalty.

CASE STUDY: THE ZEGNA GROUP – THE POWER OF GUIDING PRINCIPLES[4]

"A great family makes a great company, a great company makes a great family."

Gildo Zegna, CEO

The Zegna Group is one of the most dynamic and successful companies in Italy. It has a US$600 million turnover from its business as a world leader in luxury men's clothing. The company is debt free and is now run by the fourth generation of the Zegna family. The remaining third-generation sibling, Angelo, acts as president for the firm. Ownership is equally divided between two family branches, with two cousins (one of them Angelo's son) acting as co-CEOs.

The company was founded in 1907 by Angelo Zegna and taken over by Ermenegildo Zegna in 1923. Ermenegildo's strong

---

[4] See www.zegna.com.

environmental and social patronage was embedded into the firm from the start. Through his influence, the company built hospitals and also a beautiful scenic road, the Panoramica Zegna in Trivero, Piedmont. They also reforested mountain slopes with 500,000 conifers, rhododendrons and hydrangeas, to bring new life to the mountains above Trivero. Ermenegildo's values were about leading in an ethical and humane way and using technology to implement a modern social vision. His children and grandchildren are today expanding this extraordinary environmental project. Today, fourth-generation Laura Zegna oversees the company's values and mission, which is to promote environmental education and encourage direct contact with nature. In 1993, she opened a 100 square kilometre reserve of meadows and forest, known as Oasi Zegna.

One of the secrets of their success is the family's ability to follow their founders' guiding principles. As second-generation Aldo Zegna told employees at the company convention in 1999, a year before he passed away:

> "The virtues of our father, Ermenegildo, did not only include intelligence and great vision but also perseverance, dedication and coherence, and this is the legacy that Angelo and I received which has fuelled and guided our activity. Being able to predict the future, having intuition, working courageously with persistence as well as having a sensitivity for social causes are the messages which I give you now when our working life is about to close."

The fully integrated clothing business, which controls the entire supply chain from raw materials to customer purchase of the finished item, is built on strong values and traditions that were clearly defined by the first generation, and adapted and redefined successfully by the younger generations. According to Anna Zegna:

> "For the Zegnas, it all started with a social commitment to the small community and the people of Trivero. We pass these values on to our children from generation to

generation and it is the duty of the family to bring these values to the company. Thus, the family business is a point of reference of values."

The co-CEOs, Gildo and Paolo, define those family values as:

- self-respect
- discipline
- hard work
- honesty
- trust

Having clarity around those values that drive the family and the business – their roots, authenticity and values – has been the most vital success factor for the Zegna family business. This has provided a clear vision for each generation, who respect those traditional guiding principles but also understand the importance of entrepreneurial innovation to drive the business forward and to diversify and grow. This clarity of values and vision has meant the younger generations are confident about how to make decisions, i.e. through transparency and professionalism, through the board of directors. The board consists of third-generation brother Angelo Zegna, three members of the fourth generation and a trusted non-family member, Marco Vitale, who has been with the firm since the second generation and helped facilitate the succession of the third and fourth generations. There are, of course, different personalities, opinions and views, but they are melded together successfully and productively by the insightful, forward-looking ethos of the original founder.

How to Identify the Values of Family and Business

It can be a daunting task to determine the core values of a family and a family business. The following is a series of questions that the leading family members of the business could ask to help them articulate their guiding principles.

QUESTIONNAIRE: WHAT ARE THE VALUES OF YOUR FAMILY BUSINESS?

- What's your hallmark value? What do customers, suppliers, etc., know you for?

- What values run through the 'veins' of your family business?

- Which traditions do you follow as a family? What do you believe in?

- Why are you in business together? What do you want to achieve?

- What future do you envisage for the business?

- How should staff, customers and service providers to the business be treated?

- How should those involved in the business behave? (Remember, actions have more impact than words – how you behave will define your true values.)

- Which values drive and underpin that behaviour?

- Do your family's actions align with what you say in your values statement?

- What happens if someone behaves contrary to those values?

- What makes your family business special?

- How are decisions about acquisitions, investments, strategy, etc., assessed as to their fit with your family values?

- How do you record how well the family/board/management/ staff are upholding the family's values? Do you reward those who perform best from a values-driven perspective? How so?

- How do you ensure that family values are passed down through the generations? For example, would it be through ethical wills (i.e. letters, biographies, video messages from one generation to another) or through the family charter?

- How do you keep the entrepreneurial spirit of the founder alive? Have you embedded entrepreneurial values and a drive to innovate and pursue opportunities into the culture of the business?

Leading on from the questionnaire above on general values, it would be helpful to give family members 'homework' to do on this topic. Below are a number of exercises that will encourage family members to think carefully about their contribution to and role in the business, now and into the future. While you can decide how best to administer these exercises, you could, for example, hold a 'think-in' day and incorporate these exercises and discussions into a wider discussion on the plans for the business.

EXERCISE: PRIORITISING FAMILY VALUES

1. Ask each family member to summarise his or her own values and brainstorm words that sum up their motivations under specific headings. For example:
   Family life: nurturing, kindness, politeness, courtesy, generosity.
   Business/professional life: honesty, reliability, attention to detail, ambition, determination, dedication.
   Personal life: dedication, ambition, honesty, kindness.
   Social responsibility: fairness, ethics, integrity, community.

2. Decide which family values are the most important. You might choose from the following list of values:

   Honesty, trustworthiness, loyalty, harmony, hard work, tenacity, perseverance, kindness, environmental awareness, treating all employees like family, generosity, celebrating achievements, respect, integrity, modesty, independence, innovation, accountability, tolerance, prudence, openness, empathy, enthusiasm, quality, learning, performance.

EXERCISE: CHALLENGING ONE FAMILY VALUE

Choose an issue that might challenge one of your chosen values. For example, 'Integrity'. Discuss how you might maintain the appropriate value-driven behaviour in the face of that challenge.

EXERCISE: MATCHING VALUES AND BEHAVIOUR

In order to have credibility with employees and customers alike, we need to have integrity, which means behaving in a way that is consistent with our values.

Write down sets of key values and then the behaviours/actions that are driven by those values. For example:

Values	Behaviours
Inclusion and belonging	Ensuring that everyone's ideas and contributions are heard, considered and valued.
Quality customer service and strong performance	Respect, listening to feedback, sufficient review processes.

EXERCISE: FAMILY HERITAGE DAY AND SHARING EXPERIENCES

Hold a family heritage day to educate the whole family about the history and heritage of the family business. This will help to engender a sense of belonging and pride across the generations.

- Share the history of the business. When was it founded and how did the founder take it from the 'light bulb moment' to where it is today? What early obstacles were overcome? How did it rely on its values to build resilience?

- Ask retired family members to share their experiences. Ask them to recount positive memories and stories in which family values emerge.

- Invite younger family members to comment on how they might build on that heritage themselves and how their behaviour fits with the family's values and actions (such as philanthropy). Ask them about what motivates them to get involved.

- Record as much of these valuable interactions as possible.

Communicating the Values of Your Business

In order to maximise the benefits of having strong shared values that permeate your business culture and positively impact how all stakeholders engage with and perceive your business, you must communicate those values clearly.

It's also important for staff to understand how to behave according to the values of the business. With this in mind, is it recommended that you:

1. Draft a Values Statement for approval by the family council (see **Chapter 6**).
2. Include the Values Statement in a variety of company materials and documents, such as induction manuals, on the company intranet site, in presentations and briefings, and so on.
3. Praise and reward staff who are exemplary at behaving according to those values and write about it in the company newsletter, showcasing how those staff members have used the values to inform their decision making and actions. Invite staff members to nominate others.
4. Hold a monthly or quarterly competition in which employees are invited to submit photos of those values in action.
5. Ensure that management is well versed in those values and their importance to the business and its culture. It's vital that they understand the values so they can effectively engage employees.
6. Ensure that individual objectives listed in job descriptions are aligned with the company values.
7. Gather external feedback from suppliers, customers, etc., to gauge how strongly your values inform your actions from their perspective. What words might they use to describe your business and values? Can they give examples of witnessing your values in action?
8. Enable three-way communication between senior management, staff and family members. Encourage staff members to submit feedback and suggestions to senior management to pass on to the family council and aim to implement those suggestions where possible.

CASE STUDY: M I DICKSON LTD – THE VALUE OF VALUES[5]

M I Dickson had its commitment to strong shared values rewarded in winning the 2010 Coutts Prize for Best UK Family Business in the £5–£25 million turnover category.

The values espoused by the company took time to emerge and be articulated clearly. Aided by family business expert Lucy Armstrong, the co-owners, Michael and Christine, were encouraged to address a number of vital questions, such as 'What do you want for the business?' and 'If it was one of your children – what would your ambition for it be?'

This led to the realisation that at the very core of their business was a shared sense of strong family values and pride in the family's achievements. As Michael says, "I believe our business has, over the years, become part of the fabric of our region and can lay claim to a distinct personality based on quality products, a brilliant workforce and strong family values."

Stemming from their work with Lucy Armstrong, they set up a family council and drafted a family constitution to enable other family members to stay informed and involved and to guide the board about family values, strategy and purpose.

It was this active promotion of the core values that impressed the judges of the Coutts award. Roger Pedder, National Chairman of the evaluation committee, commented as follows:

"As a successful second and third-generation family business, the things that impressed the evaluation committee about M I Dickson included:

- the family's commitment to remain in family ownership for future generations;

- the company's clear strategic vision and ability to diversify in a competitive market;

---

[5] Dickson, M. Interview with author (July 2013).

- the strength of the family's values and culture which run throughout the business in everything they do and features heavily in their branding;

- the family's well-organised governance, which has helped smooth succession and keeps the family informed and connected to the business via a family constitution, family council and board representation;

- the company's willingness to embrace non-family management and advisers in order to drive the business forward and support family succession; and

- the family's strong approach to community involvement and charitable giving through the Dickson Family Charitable Trust."[6]

Michael further notes, "The business has evolved over the years to meet the changing expectations of a growing customer base. Family values are fundamental to our business model, which succeeds thanks to the energy, commitment and professionalism of a loyal staff."

Another one of their values is serving the community. Michael Dickson has long been passionate about the importance of local family businesses within the community: "I'd banged on for years about how soul-destroying it can be when visiting towns around the UK: they're all so predictably the same with the inevitable overbearing presence of the usual national and multinational brands. Family businesses largely fail to survive past second generation and I'd never really considered the pathology behind that demise until speaking with Lucy Armstrong, a specialist in family business matters. It proved something of an epiphany when I realised that that was a real danger our business faced if I didn't take some significant steps to address the situation."

---

[6] "'And the Winner Is...' M I Dickson Limited Wins the Coutts Prize for Family Business", *Dicksons Newsblog*, 10 June 2010.

The need for core values was well understood by Michael, but even he did not grasp the full extent of applying those values: "In practical terms we had to have buy-in from my sister Chris and daughter Elena, the working family members, but also the belief and support of wider family who would be heirs to the business. Looking back, I think it's fair to say I was a little sceptical about this because my other three children all had their own careers, and our younger sister, Dorothy, had lived in France for many years. I thought that we could expect little more from them than a nostalgic attachment to the business, while Christine was sceptical almost to the point of dismissiveness."

Lucy volunteered to speak with each of them privately about the possibility of forming a family council. "I thought this was the only way to open a dialogue because I didn't want to prejudice their views in any way or influence what they wanted to do. We had to have willing participants in this endeavour because ultimately council would be instructing a non-family board, probably via a non-family MD. I remember saying to Lucy early on in our discussions, 'I don't have a problem with you talking to them to see if they want to come along to the odd meeting, but it's not really their problem.' She replied, 'Michael, when you drop dead, it will immediately become their problem.' And I thought, 'Well, that's one way of putting it!'

"I need not have worried, and was frankly amazed by the pride the family showed in the company and I'm delighted to say our council has been running and developing for over four years with their willing input and support and Lucy's ongoing input. This is no panacea, of course, but there's far more chance of our business being sustained and continuing to develop if family shareholders 'get' how it operates, appoint and monitor a professional board, set its goals and ensure it buys into our family values. We can continue to not only protect people's jobs but create new opportunities, provide ongoing family income, protect family wealth and encourage family cohesion."

When a clear set of values forms the foundation of the company's vision, this is something that will unite family members and non-family members alike. As Michael puts it: "Having the wider family commit to the company in this way has been crucial, but our staff value working in a family business environment because they see an organisation that won't make decisions based on short-term rewards and that offers them a degree of job security that's not as readily apparent in the corporate sector. I believe they buy into our vision and cherish the more personal relationship they have in a family business environment. This 'personal' dimension to our business is important to our customers and suppliers and we believe it delivers a competitive advantage."

3. A Shared Vision

The Zegna family (as featured in a case study previously) provides a good example of how strong guiding principles and values can enable a business to flourish. However, as well as clarity about what the business is and what stands for (values), the business also needs to know where it is headed and anticipate what is yet to come (vision). It is from the fundamental values and aspirations of the business that the vision will emerge.

A **vision statement** is a declaration of what the business wants to achieve or accomplish in the medium and long terms. A good vision statement will inform and inspire the daily operations of a business and help to shape strategic decisions. For example, Coca-Cola's vision serves as the framework for their 'roadmap' and guides every aspect of their business by describing what they need to accomplish in order to continue achieving sustainable, quality growth:

"• **People:** Be a great place to work where people are inspired to be the best they can be.
• **Portfolio:** Bring to the world a portfolio of quality beverage brands that anticipate and satisfy people's desires and needs.

- **Partners:** Nurture a winning network of customers and suppliers, together we create mutual, enduring value.
- **Planet:** Be a responsible citizen that makes a difference by helping build and support sustainable communities.
- **Profit:** Maximize long-term return to shareholders while being mindful of our overall responsibilities.
- **Productivity:** Be a highly effective, lean and fast-moving organization."[7]

How to Identify the Company's Vision

In gathering the information necessary to draft a vision statement, the family members should first answer a series of questions to determine their thoughts on the future direction of the business.

QUESTIONS FOR FAMILY MEMBERS IN DRAFTING A VISION STATEMENT

1. What are your ambitions for the family business? Where do you see the business in three to five years' time?

2. What markets are you in? How is the firm performing?

3. What kind of enterprise do you wish to build?

4. What do you feel good about and proud of in relation to the business?

5. Consider the successes and achievements of the business. What are its strengths?

6. What precisely do you want from the business, both professionally and personally? A long-term career? To leave a legacy behind?

7. How do you want the business to grow – rapidly, through external funding (giving away equity to non-family members), or organically, by reinvesting profits back into the company? Is yours a short-term or a long-term vision?

[7] www.coca-colacompany.com/our-company/mission-vision-values.

8. What will the business look like when it is either (a) ready to be handed over to the next generation or (b) ready to be sold? Define your exit strategy clearly. Would you rather sustain the business through the next generation and live off a share of the profits, or sell it and profit from the sale price?

The questions above will elicit a lot of very helpful responses from family members regarding their personal visions for the business. The next step will be to collate those findings into a single vision statement, which should be circulated among all family members for their input. It might take time to arrive at the best wording, but it will be time well spent. At the end of this process, the company will have a strong vision statement, a consensus view about the nature and ambition of the business, its future positioning and the role of the family in achieving that future. This document can be a powerful tool in terms of motivating staff, guiding decisions and successfully inducting the next generation into the business.

CASE STUDY: EPS GROUP – SHARED VISION[8]

EPS Group is a sustainable water solutions provider that was founded in 1968. It is transitioning well into the second generation and growing from strength to strength. Clarity around communication, vision, purpose and values and a solid succession plan are the secrets of its success.

The values have been entrenched in the company since day one, and the company is still driven by its values, which are: its stakeholders, innovation, sustainability, respect for people, high performance and reliability.

[8] Buckley, P., EPS Group. Interview with author (July 2013).

Based on this, the company has created a clear mission and vision statement:

"To design, build, operate and maintain sustainable water solutions, focused on the global provision of clean water for customers and their communities…to be the best place to work, our customers' partner of choice and to be the most sustainable company in our industry."

Patrick Buckley, Deputy MD, understands the power of vision to propel a family business forward: "The key thing for the second generation is our purpose. The first question that the second generation have asked ourselves is why we're involved in the company, or not involved, because some are not involved and others are…so why are we here? Is it just because it's a family business and it's just a job or do we have something more strategic to offer? And do we want to do more of the same or do we want to take the business to the next level in our careers? And then how do we conduct ourselves? Is it with the same passion and professionalism and commitment to the business that the first generation had? Or are we just going to coast it? So we have considered our whole approach in terms of how we conduct ourselves. To be fair, everybody in the second generation is interested in growing the business, is committed and passionate about their work."

A company's vision is like a torchlight, illuminating the direction and destination of the business. It can only work, however, if it is a collective vision, one that inspires everyone involved. The vision will shape decisions, goals, strategic plans, talent selection, succession choices, and so on. It will be all-encompassing and will act as the fuel to sustain the family through the hard work of running a successful business. Together with the company's articulated values, the vision will provide meaning and purpose so that it is always clear why you are doing what you do and why it is important – to you and your family – to continue to do so.

> "Dreams provide the broader psychological context within which sets of specific goals can be organized, prioritized, and invested with excitement. They work at a deeper emotional level…Dreams have the power to sustain excitement through-out people's lifetimes, and to guide their fundamental choices…"
>
> Ivan Lansberg[9]

The following exercise involves drafting your company's vision state-ment. This would be handed to family members and senior execu-tives for their input. The views would then be collated at a workshop to arrive at a shared vision statement.

EXERCISE: DRAFTING THE VISION STATEMENT

The purpose of [your company] is to _____so that

_____.

It does this by being _____because

_____ is important to us.

We aim to be _____.

Of course, while values are fundamentally embedded into the heart of the business, visions can shift with time as markets and other exter-nal factors change, as diversification and expansion into new markets becomes viable, and as new generations innovate and develop the business. It is important to remember that while the vision should be shared and clear, it should also be open to change as circumstances dictate.

In an interview with the author, Alex Polizzi (Forte hotels heir and television presenter) responded to the question, "What were the most common issues, problems and obstacles encountered in

---

[9] Lansberg, I., *Succeeding Generations: Realizing the Dream of Families in Business* (Harvard Business Review Press, 1999).

your familys' hotel business?" with a very interesting insight into the role of vision in a family business:

> "It's quite often that businesses that were successful at one point become less successful over time because the vision hasn't changed over time. You can have a model that's working very well, for example Pizza Express was incredibly successful for ages, all through the seventies and early eighties, then lost its way and became too cheap and too cheerful and it's taken a lot to turn that business around...Someone then re-envisaged the whole business and Pizza Express is now what it once was. You see that a lot, when you follow faithfully in the trenches of the ones who went before and that doesn't work because the times, they are a changing – and pretty quickly too. And one has to keep up with those changes."[10]

The key is to constantly revisit and review the vision of the business, to make sure it is still relevant for modern times.

"Keep up, innovate in every sense," advises Alex. "In the sense of communication, in the sense of what the customers want, in the sense of what you're offering and how you're presenting yourself – all of that needs to be constantly reviewed. And what I see a lot is companies who, by the third generation, have no real ideas anymore; they're just doing what they've always done. That's the most common thing I see."

This is why it is so beneficial to have a family charter or constitution that documents values, vision, mission and purpose and also the appropriate rules for 'the way things are done' in the business. It is equally vital to innovate, to be entrepreneurial, to consider the marketplace at any given time, to listen to customer feedback and build strong relationships so that the business can pivot, shift or change direction and follow new paths to its ultimate goal.

Well-managed and Understood Expectations

As part of the vision-defining exercise, family members will have spent time discussing their expectations. There might be expectations, for example, about the amount of work that members of the

[10] Polizzi, A. Interview with author (June/July 2013).

family should do and their participation levels in general. There may be expectations around roles and how to communicate with each other 'on the shop floor'. In order to know, understand and manage expectations, it is necessary to communicate, listen and discuss. Only then can there be understanding, compromise and, finally, agreement.

One of the most critical expectations has to do with leadership. Who is the key decision-maker in the family and in the business, and why? Is there a 'dictatorship' or strongly hierarchical structure where one leader tells everyone else what to do and they comply? Are there different levels of authority? How much authority does each person have? What kind of decisions need family council approval, if any? How is such a decision made? Is it based on a majority ruling? Taking a vote on every single decision would be incredibly time-consuming. So, if a democratic leadership set-up is preferred, there needs to be a balance between authority and inclusion; everyone must understand that each voice cannot be equal in business.

Alex Polizzi is quick to point out that strong leadership enables, rather than disables:

"I think businesses work best as a kind of benevolent dictatorship…a traditional hierarchical structure where the managing director makes the decisions, backed up and aided in that decision-making process by the board and COO and all the rest. But ultimately the final responsibility for any decision rests with the MD. I think there are businesses where everyone thinks their voice has equal weight and it just doesn't.

"Just going back to my experience, my grandfather had a successful business; however things went wrong as he got too old (because he probably should have stepped aside earlier). My uncle and my mother currently work together but my uncle is very much the boss of the company, and I think that is a scenario that works much better. You need someone to call the shots ultimately and someone to point the finger at when things go wrong. That's the other thing, otherwise everyone is: 'Well you said,' 'No you said', and 'Well I wanted…' When things are good nobody cares who makes the decisions, it's when things go sour that suddenly it becomes very important. That's why having that structure and responsibility is so key.

"That's why this business dictatorship is a good analogy, because you have to say, 'It's my way or the highway'. It's very cohesive to have that figure that everyone can coalesce around. I just don't believe there's a communal way of doing things in businesses. Even a business like John Lewis, where all the staff are shareholders, still has a finance director and someone who has to make the tough decisions. I think that really does help. Basically, it helps to have someone to blame and someone to praise.

"My mother always says she recognises absolutely that she is a junior partner to my uncle and that's very helpful; everyone knows where they stand."[11]

Another set of expectations that can cause conflict are those around succession and who is expected/expects to take over the running of the firm once the current owner leaves or dies. No member of the next generation should automatically assume that he or she will be the one to take over. It could be that his or her sibling is the chosen successor or, indeed, that there will be no successor because the founder/current leader wishes to sell the business. It is vital, therefore, for everyone to know and understand what everyone else wants from the business.

Alex Polizzi is eloquent on this point, also:

"Be very clear about what everybody wants out of the business; that's the most important thing to avoid: conflict. If the parent gets out, they probably want to get out with some money. That's something that the younger generation need to understand.

"I generally side with the generation who've built up the business because they really have sacrificed and experienced deprivation and difficulties. Normally, if the younger generation want to run the business, it's because it's been successful and it's in quite good nick. There seems to be this feeling of a God-given right and that every parent must want to hand their business on to their child, and that's so far from the case.

---

[11] Polizzi, A. Interview with author (June/July 2013).

"It's important to separate out goals; not to expect everybody to do everything. Give each member of the family an area of responsibility that is commensurate with their abilities.

"I think the problem with family businesses is an inherent one. You may have four members of the family involved; two or three who are good at one thing and one who's good at another. You may have one child who isn't involved in the business at all but still wants to reap the benefits its success. It's a very difficult one to judge and get right.

"I think the most important thing is to be very clear about what everyone's job description and responsibilities are and the expectations everyone has in the company. There's no point in having three people who'd like to sell and three who'd like to grow and build… ultimately those are contrary desires which can build tension."[12]

How to Manage Expectations Effectively

To manage expectations effectively, it is vital that family members:

- Openly discuss their exact expectations in terms of what they want from the business, both professionally and personally.
- Understand the decision-making process, who can make decisions and when they might expect to be included and involved in that process. While input and inclusion are important, there is a fine line between the value of multiple voices and the input 'noise' that can affect the leader's ability to take a decision and act on it quickly.
- Discuss and come to an understanding about expectations around involvement, participation, working hours, roles, responsibilities, rights, ambitions, vision, privacy, etc.
- Know and respect each other's core competencies and areas of expertise and, in doing so, effectively delegate to the appropriate family member when necessary. Responsibilities can be shared but need not be equal. It is far better to share based on skills and strengths than to try to share everything equally, which can cause problems. It's important to encourage families and children to voice their opinions, but also to understand how influential (or not) those opinions will be in the grand scheme of things.

[12] *Ibid.*

CASE STUDY: EPS GROUP – EXPECTATIONS

We were introduced to Patrick Buckley, Deputy MD of EPS Group, in an earlier case study. He argues that the most important areas for the second generation are having clarity about expectations, vision and values, knowing how they are going to implement them and communicating them clearly.

"The priority of the next generation coming through is to understand the expectations of others. What are other people's expectations of the business, both family and non-family? How do they manage those expectations? And then we have to have a lot of clarity around what we're about and what shape our vision is taking while the business is moving from first to second generation.

"It's about ensuring that, collectively, we have a shared vision that will take the family forward and that everyone knows where they belong in the process. The next priority is knowing strategically exactly what are we going to do about it, that is, to bring that vision to fruition. We've got the next 15 to 20 years of our careers ahead of us, so what's our priority? What's our focus for the business going forward?"

Of course, with the best will in the world, it can still be difficult not to make assumptions.

"Our succession process has of course presented some challenges and we've been through some difficulties with it. It's certainly thrown up some obstacles that we wouldn't have foreseen. You can always communicate better. One of the obstacles or difficulties you can come across is to assume you understand someone's expectations and then you realise your assumption is incorrect. Very early on all expectations need to be put on the table and everyone needs to clearly understand what others' expectations are. Then you need to find a process to identify them all, put them all into different categories and then put a process in place to deal with them quickly, because not all expectations can be met.

Some are assumed expectations and some are expectations that people may feel are due to a sense of entitlement or whatever. You need to manage those for both family and non-family."

4. Stewardship and Strategy Built on Trust and Understanding

Stewardship can be defined as "the active and responsible management of entrusted resources now and in the longer term, so as to hand them on in better condition."[13]

The ultimate objective of stewardship is to hand the business over to the next generation in a better and healthier condition than when the current owners and leaders inherited it. It is therefore built around strong governance, vision and values, and robust, well-considered succession plans and retirement provisions.

Long-term future gains are a priority in this business plan, so investment is made in the future while continuing to manage the present. For example, rather than merely prioritising short-term results like revenue, significant time and resources are invested in training, research, leadership development, succession planning, performance management and reputation building.

Stewardship works with four types of capital:

1. **Social capital:** where value is gained from strong, long-lasting relationships with suppliers, consumers, investors, employees, the local community and wider society.
2. **Family capital:** where the business is valued beyond its status as a financial resource, but as a legacy for the family's future generations.
3. **People capital:** where value is placed on the talent within the business and their skills, knowledge, commitment and loyalty.
4. **Financial capital:** the value of financial prudence and responsibility.

---

[13] Tomorrow's Company, http://tomorrowscompany.com/governance-stewardship.

Stewardship will be pursued by those who see the family business as belonging to and providing value for the next generation, its employees and the wider community; a legacy for future generations and as a shared asset for the long-term benefit of the family, rather than merely as a financial investment and provider of personal wealth and power.

This attitude, which is based on longevity and creating value for others, is good for business. It is a powerful enabler because leaders who see the business as an opportunity to create long-term value and benefit others tend to focus on long-term growth and continuous improvement and take decisions based on those positive criteria.

Stewardship Declaration

Vision and values are particularly important to families who commit to the stewardship approach to their business. The purpose of the business becomes the foundation on which to build and grow, succeed and sustain. Short-term ownership interests of individuals become less significant than the notion of doing what is good and right for the business over the long term. A sense of community and responsibility comes to the fore and leading family members must find ways to work *on* the business rather than merely *in* it.

If stewardship is part of the family vision, then it should also become part of the family constitution or charter. It is important to draft a stewardship declaration within the family charter, where asset management, dividend distribution, succession and financial planning and the obligations and responsibilities of family members are all defined. (**Chapter 6** will examine family charters in greater detail.)

In the stewardship declaration it is important to clarify:

- how long-term investment and shareholder liquidity will be balanced;
- how the philosophy of stewardship is communicated to current and future generations and ingrained in the overall vision, mission and purpose of the business;
- how success is benchmarked and measured in both financial and non-financial terms; and
- how the business supports and will continue to support the community, from fundraising to education to environmental initiatives.

The Benefits of Good Stewardship

1. **Accountability** As stewardship focuses on the future and sustainability, it promotes a strong level of accountability within a business and safeguards its assets. Accountability is an essential cornerstone of any enterprise, family-owned or otherwise. Everyone should be held accountable for their actions, performance and responsibilities. The best way to do this is by having clear job descriptions and review processes that clearly define who each individual is accountable to and what they are accountable for.

2. **Respect** Respect can only be earned by behaving in a way that is consistently honourable; by treating others as you would wish to be treated; being honest, trustworthy and accountable; by delivering what you say you will deliver and keeping your promises. Stewardship is closely aligned to core values, which foster respect by creating a well-run, open and fair work environment.

3. **Mutual Trust** This enables communication and collaboration and strengthens relationships – a vital component of working with other people effectively, be they family members, staff, suppliers, customers or partners. Strong relationships built on mutual trust and respect cement the success of the business and the family.

4. **Forward Planning** Stewardship requires focus, foresight and vision. It requires clear strategies and goals, performance measurement and review and a passion for continuous improvement. Vitally, it also requires much thought and planning around the succession process. Succession and exit planning should therefore commence at least three to five years before the current leader is ready to step down. New leaders need to be sufficiently mentored, trained and given the chance to shine and deliver. Or, if the business will be sold (and stewarded towards a valuable sale), the business needs to be sufficiently groomed to optimise value before attracting potential buyers. Any and all measures that can help to plan for the future are a welcome addition to the family business.

CHAPTER 4

Investing in Employees

Introduction

People are any company's greatest asset, and it is the retention and development of talent that enables a smooth journey towards the long-term vision of the business, reduces staff turnover and its associated costs and ultimately assures the current and future value of the company. This human capital adds far more value than processes or procedures in the long term. Good staff take care of the customers, who in turn take care of the business. Staff members who feel valued and engaged will deliver, be more creative and more productive, and will become very effective brand ambassadors. Staff members who feel undervalued will perform below par, leave a negative impression with customers and leave as soon as they can. For these reasons, it's important not to view employees as an expense, but rather as a wise investment.

In the area of employees, family businesses can actually enjoy an advantage over larger, corporate business models. The family business, which is smaller and more intimate, can provide ample opportunity to appreciate the work put in by individual employees. This can help to create a culture that recognises, respects and rewards both non-family and family employees alike. By tracking and rewarding performance, by engaging and empowering your brightest minds to participate, by unlocking potential and creating a culture with a common purpose, it is possible to build and retain a team that will take the business forward. The key to success is retention, a crucial sense of belonging and loyalty – creating a work environment in which all staff members can excel, where they feel valued and recognised, where they feel 'at home' and do not want to leave.

How Can a Business Retain Staff?

There is a very simple answer to this question: make employees happy, make them feel that their input makes a real, valuable contribution to the business, make them feel secure and reward them for work done well. The important thing to remember here is that this does not begin and end with financial compensation. Yes, money makes people happy, but there are other, more intangible things they also need in order to achieve happiness in work, such as feeling that their well-being is important to their employer, knowing their leaders have confidence in their abilities, feeling that what they do is seen and recognised and hearing a heartfelt 'thank you' when it's warranted.

At base, there are two key ways to retain staff:

1. **Talent cultivation and inclusion:** developing potential by providing the right tools and an energising environment that encourages ideas and innovation, listens to people and makes them feel valued and included. This is coupled with a culture that fosters growth and development of staff by allowing them to take on new duties and responsibilities and to receive the necessary training and development to effectively undertake these duties.
2. **Motivation:** finding out what makes each person tick and then offering them individually meaningful incentives and rewards.

1. Talent Cultivation and Inclusion

The right approach when it comes to employees is to see them as vital assets of the business that must be actively protected and encouraged to grow. It is necessary for owners and managers to work on staff relations every day, seeing it as an important part of their responsibilities. A dynamic, successful team does not just happen; it requires proactive work to create the right environment for employees to find their niche and work to their best potential. Managers can do this by fostering team spirit and by nourishing talent.

Foster Team Spirit and Create the Right Space

It's important to create a healthy and productive working environment. This means tackling two elements: the physical environment and the atmosphere that pervades it.

The place of business should be a pleasing space in which to work, with the right up-to-date equipment and facilities to enable staff to do their work effectively. This should be supported by strong, effective leadership and effective training and development. It's important to appreciate that physical space matters. A bright and colourful interior design, for example, will have a far more positive impact on creativity and productivity than a dull, bare workspace. From the colour of the walls to the healthy ergonomic layout of the working environment, the workspace should have a logical and comfortable flow that promotes openness, congregation and shared conversation, where people feel good when they walk through the door in the morning.

Secondly, this well-thought-out workspace needs to have a good atmosphere. A happy workforce is a productive one, so it is essential that there is positivity in the workplace. A sense of humour is always a very helpful addition to any workplace, provided it does not lead to excessive informality which could cause offence to some staff. It usually requires just the 'little touches' to create the a good working atmosphere, such as including praise for employees on the walls, suggestion boxes, employee of the month awards, making Friday a 'free cake for employees' day, or ordering in pizza for lunch to mark an achievement. In this way, the workplace becomes a pleasant, fun and motivational environment where 'wins' are acknowledged and celebrated. Promoting this sort of collegial atmosphere can generate a spark that jumpstarts the creative process, boosting morale and trust and enabling people to perform better and achieve more.

While positive and fun surroundings and activities boost productivity, creativity and loyalty, having a people-oriented manager with strong interpersonal skills at the helm can also encourage staff retention. According to a recent survey by market research firm Ipsos, staff with managers with an "above average" sense of humour are 90% more likely to remain in their jobs and still be there a year later, compared to 77.5% with managers with "average" or "below average" senses of humour.[1] Similarly, the Great Place to Work Institute has

---

[1] Quoted in Rigby, G. *From Vision to Exit* (Harriman House, 2011).

revealed that providing a "fun environment" classifies 81% of companies as "great" rather than merely "good".[2] People don't want to leave places where it is great to work, where camaraderie is nurtured and there is a strong sense of belonging.

> "You can easily recognise a productive workplace – it's the one where the people look as though they're having a good time."
>
> Brian Chernett,
> Founder of the Academy for Chief Executives

Nourishing Ideas and Promoting Inclusion

Just as people need care and attention within an encouraging environment in order to thrive, so too do their ideas. This is important because in today's smart economy, ideas fuel change and growth, particularly in a business world that is changing at an exponential rate. It is the hallmark of successful organisations, with loyal and committed teams, that they promote, encourage and hear their employees' ideas.

The key to getting the best from your human capital is by:

- Fostering a culture from the top down where good ideas are encouraged and staff feel listened to.
- Listening to employee ideas, communicating with them and fostering an environment of inclusion. Ensure your welcome message gives employees a sense of ownership/input over decision-making processes and the ultimate vision of the firm.
- Providing an environment and creating a culture that stimulates innovation and provides a platform for individual and team creativity. An ideas box can be set up in the workplace and any staff ideas that are implemented from this box that result in cost savings or increased sales should be credited to the employee/manager and they should be appropriately rewarded.

All ideas should be welcomed and 'greenhoused', all input should be valued, and all creators of those ideas should be included and involved. Doing so can have significant positive effects on growing businesses. Not only does the nourishment and encouragement of

[2] www.greatplacetowork.net.

ideas uncover solutions around the efficiency and quality of processes and products (and thereby creating a competitive advantage and boosting profitability), it also creates an energetic and positive team atmosphere, which in turn promotes loyalty and lowers staff turnover.

Siobhan Browne, Managing Director of Siobhan Browne and Associates Limited, advises: "Firms who are good in this area constantly encourage staff to make suggestions, no idea is a bad idea, and all ideas are openly and positively received. Not all will progress to implementation, but the person with the idea is applauded for the input and rewarded where it gets to implementation. Peer recognition is very important here, so telling staff about a team member's good new idea is motivational. Another excellent idea is having the person whose idea it is do a short presentation and/or talk to the team about the idea and how they feel it might be progressed. This allows for a forum for good, effective, respectful critiquing of the idea by peers and generally leads to sorting out any snags that could arise at an early stage."[3]

Furthermore, listening to their ideas and enabling employees to grow professionally and personally in their work through mentoring and training creates a flexible and committed workforce, which in turn gives the company greater stability and sustainability. Employees who are respected and fulfil their potential in their workplace work better and smarter and, crucially, stay longer.

The second facet of recognising employees' contribution is to foster a culture of **inclusion**. Employees who feel included, involved, responsible and autonomous will work better than those who don't feel the same sense of participation. If employees (both family and non-family) are empowered to contribute by making decisions, creating products and providing customer service, they will have a strong sense of personal ownership that will strengthen their commitment to the family company.

By bringing non-family employees into the fold, family businesses can create an environment of 'extended family', which non-family businesses will find difficult to rival. This is a special feature of the family business and should be used to its best advantage by actively working to create a working environment in which staff members feel safe, inspired and valued.

[3] Browne, S. Interview with author.

CASE STUDY: M I DICKSON LTD –
PROMOTING A GOOD EMPLOYEE CULTURE

As we have seen in previous chapters, Michael Dickson, MD of one of South Tyneside's most successful family firms, which is now run by the second and third generations of the Dickson family, has always created a welcoming atmosphere for non-family members.

"Everyone receives a personal birthday and Christmas card with complimentary (tax paid) vouchers. We routinely mark the marriages and births amongst our workforce and always communicate with anyone who's bereaved.

"The store of the month sees staff enjoy a subsidised night out; we also have an award for employee of the month and mark long service. We publish a professionally printed bulletin each quarter that's informative but unmistakably light-hearted. These gestures are important but we can't take employee goodwill for granted and while salary levels have to be informed by harsh financial realities, we have looked hard at peripheral staff benefits and profit-related bonus payments to promote the idea of common purpose. We're also considering replacing twice yearly staff engagement surveys with a staff council to further encourage constructive dialogue with our workforce."

This feeling of camaraderie and of being 'part of the family' was brought home when Michael's sister and co-owner, Christine, passed away recently.

"Hundreds attended her funeral and we closed retail shops and what factory functions we could so that those staff who wished could be present. One long-serving employee who has worked for us since their school days told me losing Christine was like losing his mum.

"We are a close knit team, and I think those solid family credentials were recognised in the Coutts UK Family Business of the Year (£5m–£25m category) 2010 and latterly when our Diamond Jubilee celebrations as a family business culminated in a visit to our factory headquarters by the Princess Royal."

That close-knit culture has paid dividends for the M I Dickson team: not only have they been able to rally round and support each other during tough times, they also have a very ingrained sense of loyalty, which has enabled the company to grow and achieve a strong competitive advantage.

2. Motivation

People are different, and they respond differently to motivational factors. It is not the case that a business can draw up a template of motivation and apply it rigidly to all staff members. This simply would not work. What will work, however, is fostering an interest in and care for every employee's well-being and encouraging managers to get to know their staff well enough to know and understand what truly motivates them. Interestingly, in recent studies the level of interest from management in an individual's level of well-being was found to be the most engaging and motivating factor of all, rated even above pay or career development.[4] As well as motivating staff, showing that you care about their well-being can reduce the number of days off, reducing downtime and sick pay.

Motivational factors largely fall into four main areas or types, and it is a key task of management to figure out which motivation type will work with a particular member of staff:

1. The nature of the work
2. Personal achievement and development
3. Recognition, appreciation and reward
4. Money (financial security)

---

[4] For example, see "What Drives Employee Engagement and Why it Matters", Dale Carnegie Training White Paper, 2012.

1. The Nature of the Work

Generally, the work itself is a prime source of motivation. To feel engaged, people need to be aware of:

- what is expected of them;
- how their role fits into the wider organisation, i.e. how their role makes a difference and contributes to the overall objectives and vision of the company; and
- how the company is performing.

Staff who are informed about what's going on within the business, how the business is doing and where they fit into it are more likely to provide a better and more focused service to customers than those who don't have access to such information. As such, **communication** can positively or negatively affect such critical success factors as repeat custom, customer loyalty and spending per customer.

While challenging work is stimulating, **the workload should be manageable** to avoid counterproductive stress.

As well as being approachable on a daily basis, management should also meet regularly with staff to help them optimise performance. The staff members should create results-led personal action plans and outline in the meeting how they intend to implement those actions and achieve those results before the next meeting. It is up to the managers to outline how they can support those priorities, keep the role interesting and, should the actions or results not be achieved, coach the member of staff and/or discuss how to make the action plan more achievable. Gradually, the staff member will solve his or her own problems and meet targets without the need for intervention or the same level of guidance. Encourage open and frequent conversations with employees to head-off problems that could lead to disengagement.

HOW TO MOTIVATE THROUGH THE NATURE OF THE WORK

- Ensure that staff are truly engaged in the work they are doing and find it interesting.
- Provide people with opportunities to meet and talk to the right clients and/or team members so they can have a true impact on the business.

- Provide clear objectives that are fully aligned to the overall business objectives, showing how their individual objectives will be key in achieving those of the business.
- Outline expectations and set priorities.
- Review goals regularly and discover how you can help, and enable contribution and offer support.
- Provide the gift of awareness to your staff. Give regular updates of what's going on. Don't shield them from challenges – include them in the conversation.
- Match expectations. Give people realistic expectations of what they're going to get out of a role. Ensure people are clear about what is expected of them and what the rewards will be.

2. Personal Achievement and Development

Personal fulfilment in one's career and the company's commitment to enabling personal growth are key motivational factors. People who can identify a long-term opportunity for themselves in working for your business are more likely to stay. Commit to designing a long-term career structure for people and they will commit to your business over the long term. As Siobhan Brown notes, "Anecdotally, staff will often comment that in smaller organisations they were afforded the opportunity to undertake more responsibility sooner and have broader roles at an earlier stage in their career than might arise in a larger, more bureaucratic firm. Also, staff in smaller firms can be afforded an opportunity to observe and experience some activities and responsibilities under supervision that would not arise in a larger firm."[5]

How to Motivate through Personal Achievement and Development

- Uncover people's self-actualisation drivers. Where do they see themselves in five years' time and how can you help them realise their career aspirations within your company?

---

[5] Browne, S. Interview with author.

- Invest in staff training and development. Help people to develop their talent and key strengths rather than focusing on their weaknesses. This investment is not purely financial. Afford staff the opportunity to be involved is and to observe activities that other senior staff are doing as a means of developing them. Allow staff to be part of discussions on business planning and problem solving.

- Hold regular one-to-one meetings not only to discuss plans of action and the future needs of the business, but also to discuss people's own performance, career journeys and training needs. Encourage staff to actively participate in these meetings, perhaps by rotating the chairing of the meetings to give staff the experience of doing this. Task staff with taking and circulating minutes of meetings for development.

3. Recognition, Appreciation and Reward

From commission and bonuses to share option schemes, gym membership, firm-sponsored dental cover and health insurance, and gifts that reward good work (such as bottles of champagne, extra holidays, shopping vouchers, air miles, and so on), there are myriad ways to reward good performance. Of course, smaller businesses might struggle to give financial rewards, but there are inexpensive ways to make staff feel appreciated, even if it is simply saying 'thank you'. Other, non-financial alternatives might include offering options such as:

- The ability to buy and sell annual leave: as long as business is not disrupted, staff could buy or sell between three and five days' worth of holiday entitlement per year, provided they do not sell any of their core statutory entitlement of 20 days per annum.
- The ability to buy discounted benefits offered by the company at group discounted rates, such as extra dental or medical insurance, life assurance or critical illness cover. Consider providing cost-effective additional benefits to staff, such as an employee assistance programme which provides a range of excellent counselling and advisory services to staff and typically costs €30 per employee per annum to provide as an employer.

- Life assurance, when bought by an employer at a group rate, is a fraction of the cost of personal life assurance – many employers we interviewed have been pleasantly surprised at the actual cost of benefits such as this.
- TaxSaver travel tickets.
- Cycle to Work Scheme.
- Partnering with employees to share the costs of further education programmes.

How to Motivate with Incentives and Rewards

- Recognise achievements by praising, rewarding and promoting your team based on performance. Tell people when they have done a good job. Hold regular employee appreciation events to congratulate and thank top performers, motivate staff and share your vision.

- Incentivise staff with a range of performance-related incentives, such as flight tokens, discount cards, group 'away days' or match/concert tickets. These are great incentives, but it is important to be mindful of the BIK (benefit in kind) implications of any schemes such as these. Under current Revenue rules, any gift in excess of €250 per annum is typically subject to BIK.

- Provide staff with the opportunity to share in the success of the business through shares and share options. This gives talent a vested interest in enhancing the performance of the company and also a good reason to stick around to realise the value of their shareholding. These are costly and complex schemes to put in place, so the likely benefits need to be carefully considered, but in certain environments they are a critical factor in retaining key talent. Note that expert tax and legal advice is necessary when considering setting up any such schemes.

- Ensure that you have clear measures of performance so that everyone will know when bonuses or incentives have been earned. Performance-related rewards can only be effective

> where they are linked to overall company goals, are jointly agreed and where they can be measured.
>
> • Align goals and related rewards with company goals and customer feedback. Encourage customers to tell you who they think the best performers are. Such feedback can improve customer referral rates and satisfaction rates simultaneously.

Siobhan Browne further notes that, "All evidence will say that the manner and timing of the recognition is the key. If, for example, a staff member assisted in a big event in March, then at the time of the event they should be thanked and not have to wait until December for their review to be thanked. An MD of a large Irish Plc I spoke with recently advised me that the most motivating thing they can recall from all their years of work was being given a case of a wine they particularly liked by their company CEO the week after they organised a large successful company conference. It made a huge impact because it was done at the time of the event and it was personal – it was a wine they liked so it showed some thought and effort on the part of their boss to make the gift personal to them."[6]

4. Money (Financial Security)

There can often be a perception that paying more to staff means a higher base cost and so less profits for the company. However, paying well can have the opposite effect, not only by encouraging loyalty and reducing staff turnover, but also by boosting performance and productivity, which in turn increases profit margins. In essence: pay more and you can make more, both in terms of products and revenue. In addition, employers often forget the hidden costs of having to hire, such as the time and expense of the recruitment process, the time the new employee spends getting up to speed at the job and all the knowledge and skill that has been lost by a person leaving.

The best way to do this is to ensure that your bonuses or sales commissions are competitive. Know what your competition is paying and offer a good, market-rate benefits package that stacks up

[6] Browne, S. Interview with author.

well in comparison to the competition. You'll be able to afford to pay higher commissions to those bringing in higher sales income, increasing your profit margins, while the bigger incentive will motivate your team to perform better and produce more sales/leads/units, and so on. Consider increasing bonuses on a grading scale based on achieving specific targets.

For clarity, 'commission' refers to staff directly involved in sales roles and is typically a formula whereby, on achieving certain levels of sales, certain levels of commission are paid. Firms that are good at sales don't place any cap on commission as their view is that, as long as you earn more for the firm, you are entitled to earn more for yourself.

Of course, not all roles in a firm are focused on direct sales and so a firm that applies a bonus system must put an effective alternative in place for staff who are not directly involved in sales. Typically this is done by having an overall bonus pot for non-sales staff and having a sliding scale whereby staff who rank higher on achievement of objectives get a greater percentage bonus than staff who did not perform as well.

There are a few potentially problematic issues with commission structures and performance-related pay that should be noted:

1. They can expressly focus on the efforts of the individual, rather than the effort of the team or the company as a whole. This can create competition between individuals within a team, which has its pros and cons. The downside is that it can lead to individuals undermining their competing coworkers to improve their own sales figures or performance; the upside is that it can also provide an extra motivator for one individual to outsell or perform better than the other, and so on. To minimise this, it is key that all salespeople objectively reflect on the 'what and the how' of their role so that they are not going by a 'sales at all costs' model, which can lead to very short-term gains and poor client retention.

2. Figuring out the right timeframe on which to base incentives can be difficult. Long-term, performance-related pay may not motivate participants sufficiently, as the target and subsequent reward are too far in the future. This can lead people to concentrate on deals that are easier and quicker to close,

while incentives that are too short-term may not be in the overall interests of the company. These targets are typically annualised and some firms may make payments on a quarterly basis against them and do an overall balancing of the payments at year end.

In order to overcome these obstacles, companies should:

- Provide team/company targets and bonuses as well as individual ones to all staff. The team target might be to sell a whole range of goods or services within a certain time period, with a team bonus shared out evenly between team members if the target is reached.
- Provide top performers with team leader roles in which they are responsible for both ensuring that the team delivers its principal objectives and that individuals also deliver their targets. Incentivise and reward such leaders by paying extra commission on the sales that their team members make.
- Provide larger incentives for winning larger, longer-term deals, therefore adequately rewarding people based on the difficulty of the sale and the subsequent increased effort required to close such a deal. Staff members are then more likely to aim to close a mixture of both short-term and long-term deals.
- To accommodate and recognise the importance of non-financial incentives, such as training and development, take into consideration the time of year individuals will be training so that their commissions are not adversely affected by dips in productivity that personal development might cause.

Shares used to be a discretionary incentive scheme for key senior executives. However, these days share-ownership is sometimes extended to *all* employees. It is up to each company to decide who to extend share schemes to, what types of scheme to use, when to use them and why. As noted earlier, there are legal and tax issues to be considered here and good professional advice is necessary in determining how to proceed.

Many family firms confine equity share-ownership to family members only. This puts them at a disadvantage, however, when trying to recruit or retain talent if their competitors do offer share options.

If you are worried about the implications of giving shares in the family firm to non-family members, there are some good alternatives to consider, for example:

- restricted voting shares, which carry restricted or no rights to vote at general meetings but are otherwise identical to other equity shares;
- restricted transferability shares, which must be transferred back to the family when the non-family member leaves the company (or before they can be sold);
- phantom shares, which are essentially based on a cash bonus amount determined by the increase in value of notional shares; or
- percentage bonuses based on appreciation in the company's value but without ownership of shares, i.e. allowing for participation without the risks.

The provision of shares as an incentive can be complex in itself, too, as there are different ways of providing share-based incentives: through either long-term or short-term cash bonuses, which are partially deferred into shares; through market-priced options or restricted 'gifted' options; through Revenue-approved schemes only; or topped up with unapproved bespoke schemes for individuals. Unapproved schemes are used as a top-up above approved schemes once approved schemes have been maximised (for example, if it was necessary to ensure that some senior executive being headhunted into the company had a big enough equity stake to give them adequate ownership).

If performance criteria are likely to be determined by company performance rather than the performance of an individual, long-term share option plans are the most suitable because executives should only be rewarded if the business is performing well.

If you intend to provide shares as an incentive to non-family staff as well as family, you should consult with an advisor and discuss the implications of this on the family's level of ownership.

Depending on your exit strategy (see **Chapters 10** and **11**), you might wish to go one step further and create a share-ownership scheme. This is particularly relevant to family-run businesses that wish to keep the ownership of the business in the family and any company owner who does not wish to sell to a third party.

How to Motivate with Money

- Pay a good basic salary and progressive benefits coupled with competitive commissions and variable bonuses to attract the best talent.

- Benchmark pay against equivalent companies/employers in a similar industry in the marketplace to ensure terms, salary and benefits are competitive.

- Provide profit-related cash bonuses based on achieving annual or quarterly targets (individual and company-based) to encourage staff to focus on the success of the business.

- Further incentivise staff retention by enhancing the value of a cash bonus with additional shares if the employee stays with the company for the long term.

- Consider giving outstanding performers, who are at the top of their pay range, a rise in salary to reward their performance.

- Provide share-ownerships options, after discussing the consequences of them in detail with the CFO, the board and a legal representative.

Fairness

There is a risk in using some of the approaches outlined above that they could 'backfire' if *all* staff are not treated equally and fairly, i.e. both family and non-family staff members. It is essential that any and all motivational tools used are careful to treat all staff members fairly.

How to Fairly Motivate and Reward All Staff

1. **Avoid favouritism** There should be no bias towards family staff members when it comes to promotions, pay scales, work schedules or rewards. Non-family members must be treated equally to family members and expected standards should be the same for all staff.

2. **Recruit, evaluate and reward based on merit** Run the business as a meritocracy and reward fairly, based on performance and competence, without bias. All incentives, bonuses and benefits should be given to all based on set criteria, irrespective of whether someone is a family member or not.

3. **Don't provide jobs for family members just because they're family** As discussed in **Chapter 4**, the firm should only hire people (family and non-family) based on their skills, knowledge and what each individual can bring to the business.

4. **Enable any suitably qualified employee, including non-family members, to apply for top jobs** If all the managerial and executive positions are held for family members, talented and ambitious people will end up looking elsewhere and could quite likely end up working for your competitors.

5. **Ensure that management lines are clear** Employees should not be reprimanded by anyone other than the person to whom they report, and certainly not by family members who, as shareholders in the business, feel it is their right to dish out criticism.

6. **Formalise family employment** Put business relationships in writing to avoid any potential for conflict or misunderstanding. This will ensure that expectations are mutually understood with regard to remuneration, roles, responsibilities and ownership.

7. **Make remuneration fair** Pay should be the same for family and non-family carrying out similar roles, and it should be based on input and effort. Family shareholders who don't work in the business need to understand why active family members are rewarded for their efforts, while inactivity may not be rewarded. Examine market rates, ensuring that pay is based on value and that salaries are fair.

8. **Refer family members to the family constitution** (See **Chapters 5** and **6** on governance.) In this way, they can understand the fairness policy and the value of having

talented non-family managers. They will be able to read up on how family members are recruited, evaluated and promoted; how bonuses and benefits are calculated and expectations managed; who appraises family members and determines remuneration; and what happens if a family member (or any other team member) is not performing to the required standard. They will also be able to see the value of committed non-family managers and see why they are required, which will help ensure that they don't feel 'passed over' or ignored, and demonstrate why key employees should be given the chance to own shares and/or be incentivised.

9. **Differentiate clearly between the rewards that family members gain by virtue of ownership and employment** There may be benefits gained as a result of ownership that non-shareholders do not enjoy, but employment rewards must be the same for all.

10. **Ask non-family managers or third parties to appraise and evaluate the competence of family members** This is a good way to ensure that there is no favouritism and that family issues or relationships do not affect the business or the individual performance of family members.

11. **Reassure non-family staff and executives** Foster a culture of inclusion, transparency and fairness. Make opportunities at the firm open to all. They need to know that their remuneration will match what is paid by non-family firms; that autocratic owners will not overrule their management decisions; that family tensions will not affect their ability to do their job; that they have a secure job with the chance to develop, progress and participate in motivational reward structures that retain top performers. Reassure them that their efforts in growing the business will be recognised and rewarded, possibly even through an equity (or quasi-equity) stake in the company.

Human Resource Compliance

Family business is no different from any other type of business when it comes to HR compliance. This means compliance with key employment legislation and practices to ensure you protect yourself and your business against future difficulties.

There are a significant number of areas now covered by employment legislation and this section serves simply to provide a high-level summary of these for your information. It is important to ensure you seek effective expert advice from an experienced HR professional should an issue that you are unfamiliar with arise.

Siobhan Browne highlights the 10 key things you must do as an employer from an HR compliance perspective:[7]

10 KEY HR PRINCIPLES

1. Provide all employees with a contract of employment in writing within 28 days of commencing employment – although best practice is to ensure you have issued and jointly agreed the contract terms prior to commencement.

2. Put in place a clear, well-worded staff handbook with clear policies and procedures on all staff-related issues. This will be the clear reference source that you and your staff use to ensure you have a clear, shared understanding of all matters relating to employment.

3. Keep a record of all staff hours of work and annual leave and retain this record for seven years. The NERA (National Employment Rights Authority) is entitled to seek to review this at any stage if you have an inspection.

4. Statutory annual leave is 20 days per annum for full-time staff and *pro rata* for part-time staff. This is the minimum by law.

5. Staff must also be paid for all public holidays, or a part payment *pro rata* to their part-time salary if they were not scheduled to work that day.

---

[7] Browne, S. Interview with author.

6. Employers are not required by law to pay company sick pay (or maternity pay/adoptive leave pay) to any staff member. However, please ensure you are fair in how you treat staff and show no favouritism to one staff member over another.

7. Provide all staff with clear payslips each time they are paid, showing basic pay and all deductions.

8. Employers may not make any deductions from any staff wages, other than statutory deductions, without the written consent of the employee.

9. Use the probationary period to make up your mind clearly about a new employee, and ensure that you have confirmed your decision to either retain them or let them go by the 10th month of their employment to prevent a situation arising whereby they can make an unfair dismissal claim.

10. In handling all staff-related matters, ensure you approach these issues by treating the person as you would like to be treated. By acting in such a manner you are unlikely to cause difficulties for yourself as an employer.

Part III

The Business

CHAPTER 5

Governance in the Family Business

Introduction

"Governance is the guiding set of principals by which a company organises itself within the legal framework of the society in which it operates in its own bylaws."[1]

The topic of family business governance is a large one and has therefore been split into two chapters in this book. In this chapter, we will explore what corporate governance is and how good governance benefits and bolsters family enterprises. We will examine how it helps to establish clear boundaries between family and business, and how it benefits and balances the core interests of all stakeholders. **Chapter 6** will focus on the different ways to structure family governance, what to discuss and include in family meetings and family charters, and how to establish the structures and protocols.

What is 'Governance'?

There are two types of governance in a family business: corporate governance and family governance. In this context, **governance** is how the business takes on board multiple expectations, views and perceptions in order to create a consensus-based set of rules, policies and protocols to help the business run smoothly.

Corporate governance ensures that:

- the business is heading in the right direction;
- the business stays on track towards achieving its goals;
- expectations are managed; and
- roles and rules are properly assigned and abided by.

---

[1] Lansberg, I., *Succeeding Generations: Realizing the Dream of Families in Business* (Harvard Business Review Press, 1999).

Governance is about establishing a shared vision among the business, an overriding set of principles and rules that will override individual family members' interests in, and ambitions for, the business. It also promotes transparency, accountability and fairness in dealings with its stakeholders – whether they are family members, shareholders, employees, customers, suppliers, the community or the government.

For most companies, corporate governance is the only concern. However, family firms of all sizes should also consider **family governance**, the importance of which is often underestimated. Essentially, family governance is a framework that:

- defines the roles, responsibilities and rights of family members;
- outlines how the family interacts and involves itself with the business; and
- outlines how owners interact with the board and executive management.

Family governance and its structures are discussed in **Chapter 6**.

The Overlapping Needs of Family, Business and Ownership

In family enterprises, there is an overlap between three core areas of governance – **business, ownership** and **family** (see the figure below) – each of which needs to be managed.

- The **business** has capital and operational needs that must be fulfilled in order to grow into a sustainable venture for future generations. Management must therefore govern operational issues, such as finance, supplier and customer relationships, human resources, strategy, etc.
- **Ownership** must maintain adequate control of the business in order to guide it towards long-term success and sustainability. As such, their focus is on liquidity, succession, capital allocation, return on investment, strategy, etc.
- **Family** members have their own financial needs, and will have varying expectations around roles, rights and responsibilities regarding the business. They are also responsible for creating the long-term vision of the business, adhering to the business's mission, and creating a legacy for future generations. They will be focused on values, vision and goals; communication, continuity and consensus; prosperity, longevity and succession.

THE THREE-CIRCLE MODEL OF A FAMILY BUSINESS

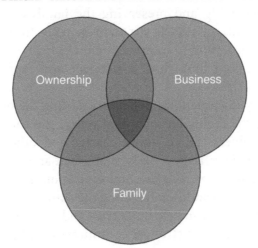

Governance does not mean opting for democracy over a hierarchical structure. While governance enables feedback and multiple opposing voices to be heard, it does not dilute ownership in any way – rather, it empowers it. There is still a hierarchy in place, just one that is better governed.

As any good professional advisor will tell you: you are not relinquishing your authority by creating governance structures. What you are doing is giving more *clarity* to your authority to ensure that it is as effective and as orderly as possible. Governance improves communication, decision making and enhances strong leadership. As such, it is a necessary tool in the toolkit of any family enterprise.

We will now explore the benefits of governance in the two equally important yet overlapping areas of ownership and the family.

Why is Governance Necessary?

Every organisation needs a set of rules to guide it – otherwise it becomes disorganised. Because family businesses can become complicated due to the family itself, it is important that governance rules for the business and the family are clear and synchronised.

A family business with good governance is far more likely to succeed over the long term. A well-governed family business is a stronger one; it is an enterprise with firm foundations that has taken steps to professionalise the business while simultaneously planning for future ownership and preserving the family's traditions and heritage. Such enterprises will see many benefits, from conflict recognition and resolution to improved management, bolstered trust, improved efficiency and, thus, a stronger and more sustainable bottom line.

By formally documenting policies regarding the operation and ownership of the family business that reflect the consensus of the family shareholders (i.e. a family charter and other governance mechanism), a clear framework is established around roles, rights, and responsibilities, as well as communication and continuity of vision and values. In addition to aiding the smooth operation of the business, such clarity can help build trust and unity within the business, which will result in stronger commitment and better decision making.

The key benefits of good governance include:

- Improved decision making and understanding as a result of enhanced communication, shared information and better internal education.
- More effective change management as a result of structured planning and policy-making procedures.
- Improved commitment, strategic awareness and unity stemming from feelings of inclusion and having one unified voice.

The Benefits of Governance for a Family Business

Good governance in a family business:

- Enables effective decision making.
- Avoids the pitfalls of unstructured decision making.
- Makes for a better and more sustainable business.
- Supports multigenerational businesses.
- Promotes commitment, strategic awareness and unity.
- Enables better relationship management due to better understanding around expectations, benefits, and roles and responsibilities.

- Fosters company-wide motivation with improved clarity of purpose and vision.
- Builds and increases trust as a result of more and clearer accountability.
- Builds and increases fairness.
- Enables effective change management.

Effective Decision Making

Governance is not just about setting rules and regulations in order to keep things organised and 'above board'. It enables effective decision making, focused on the best aspects of the business and family, to ensure that the business succeeds. Indeed, all of the core advantages of being a family business (as discussed in **Chapter 1**) – such as strong work ethic, faster decision making, and long-term sustainability – are amplified by good governance.

A key to success in business is the ability to make good, well-informed decisions – so consistently strong decision making is crucial. The only way to do that is by having access to as much important information as possible to help guide those decisions; taking on board various expert opinions and viewpoints while also listening to your own gut instincts.

After all, a business is only as good as the senior management team that runs it – and their problem-solving and critical decision-making skills. By keeping family members (who both are and are not involved in the business) informed about the business's challenges and opportunities, strengths and weaknesses, etc., the family is better able to make the right decisions and feel confident that the family members at the top of the management hierarchy have considered all angles, opinions and knowledge available to them.

As we shall see in **Chapter 6**, that's what family councils, forums and/or assemblies are for – to act as a conduit for knowledge, and to facilitate information gathering and sharing.

The family business will benefit tremendously from having clear procedures in place for sharing information and knowledge between shareholders (both active and passive). By keeping owners and other stakeholders informed about the business, better informed (and thus more effective) decisions can be made, particularly on difficult and potentially contentious matters. Nobody feels they are the 'last to know' because appropriate shareholder involvement, discussion and feedback are ensured.

Any enterprise that encourages this kind of open communication is building the ground rules and firm foundations that will help ensure the business survives across many generations.

CASE STUDY: CLARKS SHOES – MANAGEMENT VS. FAMILY SHAREHOLDERS[2]

Poor communication, lack of understanding, and disconnect between management's needs and family shareholders' aspirations can create real problems. Without strategic clarity and shareholder inclusion, even the strongest company can be troubled by crises and family disagreements.

In 1993, Clarks Shoes, a sixth-generation company and one of the UK's oldest independent family-owned businesses, came very close to being sold as a direct result of such issues.

Thankfully, once there was mutual realisation that major changes needed to be made to save the firm, the sale was averted when a family shareholder council and strengthened board became the pivotal saviours of the business. With 80% of the business owned by 350 shareholders, it was clear that representation of those multiple voices was required.

The key focal point for change was the company's communication. By improving communication, management could regain strategic clarity and shareholders could become more involved and feel included. Improved communication also enabled engagement between the owners and other stakeholders.

---

[2] Institute for Family Business, "Case Study: Clarks Shoes", www.ifb.org.uk.

One of the best ways to enable effective communication is to create a family council. In Clarks' case, this comprises 16 members elected by the 350 shareholders for four-year terms, each of whom must have a fixed and identifiable percentage of the share capital. The council meets quarterly with the board and management team and the minutes and summaries of those meetings are distributed amongst all family shareholders via the ClarksNet intranet site. Meetings between the chairman of the board and the family council chairperson also take place on a regular basis to enable a constant flow of information. The family are further represented on the board with two family non-executive directors (NEDs), also nominated by shareholders.

All of this means that the family can raise issues with the board, and vice versa; and the management team can present, discuss and share information regarding the performance of the business and future strategy with the family. Each family shareholder has a voice and can communicate their thoughts, ideas, objections, and concerns with their own family council representative.

Furthermore, as a direct result of this system of communication, clear guidelines have been defined to establish family council objectives, vision and a management/ownership division of power. This 'governance code' is regularly reviewed with external consultants in order to continue to engage owners, management and staff alike.

By establishing formal communication channels, family members and the management team have found a win–win solution – they are able to continuously share ideas, issues and aspirations in order to find common ground.

Chapter 6 will explore how to set up a family council and improve communication and decision making through other governance mechanisms.

The Pitfalls of Unstructured Decision Making

Except at the very early stages of a business's life, informal, spur-of-the-moment decision making does not work.

The interests of both the business and the family can be threatened and destroyed when communication becomes arbitrary and families unwittingly drift into damaging patterns of loose decision-making. This is a common problem in family businesses as they grow and can no longer work with informal and unstructured decision-making systems.

When governance is left too late, when the business survives purely on the energy and vision of the founder, and when independence creates a lack of accountability, the business can stall if the founder dies or becomes too busy to delegate or create a succession plan or governance structure. Good governance addresses this by providing for accountability, structure and planning.

A Better and More Sustainable Business

In well-governed companies, rules and processes are set, adhered to and managed effectively. These rules and processes are deliberated upon by the family, endorsed by the board of directors, implemented by management and followed by everyone. The result is a business with better decision making, more commitment and unity, heightened motivation and trust and fewer conflicts. Indeed, a united and committed family working together is a powerful force in business. That strength can be deepened and drawn upon if the family is well governed.

In effect, good governance maximises the business's potential to survive and thrive. Well-governed family firms can harness the power of governance to boost profits, generate jobs, develop talent, improve strategy and fundamentally sustain a successful business that serves all stakeholders.

The responsible stewardship gained through governance makes the business more viable in the eyes of all stakeholders. The business gains credibility among customers, suppliers, employees and the wider community due to the positive message good governance conveys: that this business is conscientious, cohesive and knows how to do things properly.

In an open culture where everything is considered and shared transparently – views, expectations, information, knowledge, achievements, concerns, facts and figures – there is a greater sense of unity and trust, which motivates all stakeholders to participate, work hard and stay loyal. Consequently, governance creates a perpetual loop of benefits.

Equally, there is a lot to lose without it.

A Multigenerational Business

As generations mature and both the family and the business grow, more people will be added to the ownership and management mix. As it passes down through the generations, the business and its ownership become more complex.

This complexity, however, can cause problems with decision making. What might once have been an easy decision to make can become a minefield of multiple viewpoints, assumptions and expectations. Similarly, when it comes to governance, what may have worked for the founder and his or her close family may not to serve the interests of the second generation. It can also become more difficult to transfer the values and business knowledge of the founders to future generations.

Yet the involvement of more people need not complicate things, provided that good governance procedures and processes are established when the first generation is still at the helm. Those governance procedures can evolve over time as the business and family expands and the ownership dilutes.

A common purpose and shared vision can be maintained even in large families, where disparate views on control, involvement, return on investment, etc., may be commonplace. This may get more difficult when the business gets to the third, fourth or even fifth generation, but it is still possible – and far more possible when strong family governance structures and procedures are created and executed (such as those described in **Chapter 6**). As long as a company is well-governed, it doesn't matter how many layers of complexity are added.

Each generation of the business brings with it fresh ideas about how the business ought to be run, new and varying opinions on what the business means to each individual, and what the business's strategy should be. The family governance structure must evolve with each stage, but the fundamental principles should remain in place and be clear and meaningful enough to bring order, discipline and continuity to proceedings, even in cases of family disagreement.

Good governance eases complexity and promotes multigenerational sustainability in two ways:

1. The very process and time spent as a family discussing and debating how to establish governance for the business brings a level of unity, understanding and respect to proceedings.

2. The rules established as a result of those discussions provide a solid groundwork for ensuring the success of the current and future generations, and solve any problems and issues before, or as soon as, they arise.

Commitment, Strategic Awareness and Unity

Family businesses are made up of a diverse range of individuals with varying viewpoints and different needs, expectations and skills. Boards and teams of staff are similarly diverse. Somehow, while respecting differences and listening to each other, these disparate elements must also be unified under a common vision and goal. All staff members must be able to work together cohesively and productively, with a sense of having shared interests.

A governance structure can help to achieve this necessary sense of unity within the business. It does this by putting in place a framework that:

- provides a platform for those involved and not involved in the daily running of the business to stay informed, keep in touch and ensure that their views are heard;
- listens to each stakeholder; and
- considers different opinions and ideas before determining a united consensus to deal with specific issues.

This listening approach, this opportunity for family members and stakeholders to provide feedback and to be involved in formulating ground rules and guidelines, provides two things. First, it creates consensus by describing a unified set of rules and guidelines around issues that might ordinarily be contentious. Second, it gives every family member and staff member a feeling of inclusion that leads to a strong sense of loyalty and commitment to the business and its outcomes.

Better Relationship Management

With these formal channels of communication open to everyone, all stakeholders are kept informed about business challenges and achievements. They also get to shape and stay aware of rules around employment, ownership, dividends and benefits they might receive and sacrifices they may be expected to make. This consistency and clarity generates a sense of fairness. Ultimately, by ensuring clarity around rights and responsibilities – who does what, who owns what and why – expectations can be better managed.

This is a key point. Clarity around expectations is perhaps the most important result of the open communication provided by good governance. Nothing is assumed, and fair processes are applied with consistency. This helps family businesses avoid some of the issues that can be destructive to such enterprises. After all, when families argue, it is often because of a clash over expectations and perceived rights. If those families don't have the appropriate forums to voice their concerns, it can lead to division and resentment. But as long as expectations are fully understood and well managed, and a forum for communication is provided, conflict can be avoided.

The secret is to *never* assume anything. You might have assumed certain individuals wanted to participate more or less than they actually do. You might have assumed you or someone else might be next in line to take the helm; or that shares would be spread equally; or that you would own more of the business than someone else – and been proven wrong.

It is wrong to assume. It is right to discuss things openly, gaining factual understanding rather than fostering misunderstanding.

Company-wide Motivation

As outlined in **Chapter 1**, a strong sense of shared purpose is a competitive advantage for family enterprises. This feeling of inclusion, teamwork and belonging can be captured and put into a governance system by establishing a consensus around how important the business is to the family as a whole and how success can be achieved and sustained across the generations. The drafting of this vision statement can be a bonding exercise in itself.

Once that statement is discussed, articulated and documented, it becomes a useful tool in many ways. For example, the next generation can use it to help them decide whether they wish to be involved in the family business and whether it will enable them to achieve their own goals and ambitions. Ultimately, clarity of vision can ensure that everyone is headed in the right direction together.

Trust

A governance structure builds trust among family members (particularly between those who are directly involved and those who are not but benefit nonetheless). A united family creates a stronger business. However, while it is expected that family members will trust each other, outside investors and non-family stakeholders may be suspicious of enterprises controlled by family. This can be because, for example, there have been many cases of lacking accountability and poor transparency in family firms with a high concentration of family ownership. As such, outsiders might fear that the family will abuse the rights of non-family shareholders. For that reason, family businesses will be carefully scrutinised before investors put their hands in their pockets.

Strong family and corporate governance tackles these issues in one fell swoop, as transparency and accountability are at the heart of governance structures. External investors can be assured that their interests will be kept in line by the family governance and corporate governance rules.

Accountability is also required between shareholders and other stakeholders, so policies should be set to prevent arbitrary or unfair decisions and the exploitation of non-family members' rights. This means that all key decision makers are accountable and everyone is kept in the loop. Rather than turning the business into a democracy, the hierarchical structure remains – but with policies that respect the interests of all stakeholders, the family and the business.

Fairness

Written governance rules and a formal framework promote and support fairness and transparency. Every family member's opinions and feedback should be listened to and given weight, and the consensus must rule. By inviting and listening to individual feedback, a family business can avoid divisive arguments and disagreements. This extends, of course, to all shareholders and stakeholders. While this can be a challenging task, it is a very worthwhile one.

It is necessary to ensure that disparate ideas are brought together and moulded under one banner of profitability and sustainability. For example, 'value-out' shareholders, who don't work for the business, may favour short-term returns over reinvestment; while legacy preservation and long-term growth will likely be the preference of 'custodian' shareholders who work in and on the business. This is where the benefits of governance can clearly be seen: it provides a forum for fair, effective discussion and a basis for unifying the various facets of the business in a single, agreed constitution that will guide business decisions and actions.

A key challenge facing family businesses is finding ways to fairly address the core interests of all stakeholders. By applying 'fair process', i.e. by listening to each individual and arriving at a mutually agreed consensus, decisions can be made and protected in line with that consensus. This hopefully means that each stakeholder feels their viewpoint has been heard and considered, even if it doesn't fit with the final consensus. The potential (and common) conflict regarding the critical return on investment and exit strategy is less likely to occur if the strategic vision is clear to all shareholders from the start and includes everyone's expectations around ownership and exit.

Fairness must be at the centre of good business in order to create a system of policies and structures that balances all needs and addresses the broader picture of effective rule and decision making. The critical success factor here is to enable stakeholders to raise and resolve their various interests, concerns, problems and conflicts.

While it is impossible to please all people all of the time, if the prosperity of the business is given priority and if discussion and feedback are encouraged, then those whose views differ from the consensus will still see that nobody is benefiting at the expense of others and that decisions are being made for the good of the business and of the family. This governance practice should create a sense of unity and harmony – and overarching fairness – which should in turn promote the smooth running of the business.

Effective Change Management

It is always sensible, and usually invaluable, to plan ahead as much as possible. Not every eventuality can be foreseen, but in business there is much that is predictable, such as succession and change of ownership. To this end, governance structures that assist in planning for the future are hugely beneficial to the family business. A family charter, for example, enables the family to plan today for the problems of tomorrow. (For a detailed discussion of family charters, see **Chapter 6**.) It is far easier to plan together during harmonious times than wait until conflicts arise to deal with problems, when crisis looms and emotions run wild.

It is also sensible to create governance structures, rules and procedures when the family is small (before it becomes more complex), and long before succession. Yet it's important to be mindful that governance and rules will change with the evolution of the business, from start-up to later generations of ownership. If the business proves successful and sustainable, the number of family members participating in the business will grow, and with such growth comes complexity and change.

Well-thought-out but flexible plans and strong governance guidelines will help the business safely navigate times of change. Some events will, of course, come out of the blue – people die unexpectedly, couples divorce or fall out, markets shift – but prior planning can make difficult times a good deal easier and much less stressful.

The tools of planning are quite simple:

- Use scenario planning to consider all eventualities and what you might do when faced with them. Consider situations that could impact the business or family unit and sketch out solutions and actions to execute should those situations arise. For instance, consider what processes would be followed should the founder or a senior family member/owner pass away; or what to do should a key shareholder get divorced. Will you allow ex-spouses to stay involved, sit on the board or own shares? What should happen if you receive a swift influx of assets? How might you make grants? It's a game of 'what ifs?' that allows you to identify and assess risks in advance and plan for them so that the business can react swiftly and decisively.

- Create problem-solving structures to avoid leaving issues too late to resolve. For example, a simple comments box can be an easy way to give staff a visible means of raising problems and requesting solutions. Similarly, a monthly meeting could be established to provide a specific forum for problems to be raised and discussed. The key is to create a forum of some kind where staff know they can speak freely and be heard, regardless of the issue. This promotes a feeling of equality and a sense that all problems can be shared and solved, which should give staff a sense of proportion and control.
- Stay nimble. It's never too late to make changes to improve your business, your governance structures, your relationships, and your plans. Plans should be flexible and adaptable. Never leave things to chance and hope for the best; don't hope that an informal way of doing things or an unspoken bunch of assumptions will adapt to fit changing circumstances. Be proactive and be prepared.

In this chapter, we have examined the definition and basic structure of corporate governance in relation to family businesses. We have teased out the benefits to be gained in the family business model by adhering to governance principles. It is clear that corporate governance has an important and useful role to play in any business, but especially in the family business where there is much scope for misunderstanding, conflict and disagreement.

Now that we have established that corporate governance is desirable for family businesses, **Chapter 6** will examine how the principles of governance can be introduced and implemented in the family business to aid its profitability and sustainability.

Governance Structures for the Family Business

In many ways, family businesses, with their overlapping family and business issues, are like PLCs – they are balancing the interests of management, business and shareholders.[1]

Introduction

It has been well established that best practice dictates that any conscientious, ambitious business should put in place governance structures that inform the daily operations of the business and help management to plan the future of the business. Without such structures, there is the potential for discord and division among management and employees. It is far preferable to have rigorous rules and guidelines that instruct and protect the interests of the business, be they the interests of staff members, shareholders or stakeholders. A well-run family business will always have an organised framework within which to operate, and it is the structures of corporate governance that build this framework.

In this chapter, we will examine which governance structures are most useful for the family business, and how these structures can be implemented and maintained.

The Core Governance Structures

The main components of family governance are:

1. The Family Council
2. The Board of Directors
3. The Family Constitution or Charter

---

[1] The Coutts Institute, "Governance in the Family Business: Sharing Family Business Insights".

1. The Family Council

The family council is a group of family members that comes together in a forum separate to the business. Without this separate forum for promoting the welfare of family members and resolving family issues, these matters may intrude upon the work of the board and management – at a significant cost to both the family and the business.

The family council's focus of attention is on 'the business of the family', in contrast to the board of directors' focus on 'the business of the business'. The role of the family council is to represent the interests of all generations of the family through all branches of the business, and in doing so to build a bridge between the family (shareholders) and the board of directors. The family council also provides family members with a discussion forum so that they can develop a coordinated approach to matters of importance to them.

The family council is essentially the voice of the family. It gives a voice to family members who are both employed and not employed in the business, and provides a platform to discuss family issues that impact the business (such as the return required by family shareholders/owners). The family council also gives family members the opportunity to be involved in codifying and contributing to family policies that affect existing and future generations, drafting a family charter or constitution and influencing the vision and culture of the family business. It also provides the board with a clear channel to communicate with shareholders, acting as a conduit between the two.

One of the family council's core functions is to articulate what the family's values are and what the family's vision for the business is. It also sets policies for the family (rather than for the operational side of the business, which is generally the role of the board of directors) on a number of issues, for example the distribution of perks, use of the family holiday home, resolving conflicts between family members or between family and the board, criteria and policies around the hiring (and firing) of relatives, who should be allowed to own shares, and other vital considerations such as philanthropic activities and use of the family's reputation in PR activities.

The council is also responsible for educating family members about their rights, roles and responsibilities; instilling a sense of stewardship in the younger generation; and deciding what privileges and remuneration each family member can and cannot expect. Furthermore, as a working governing body, the family council provides a forum to facilitate discussion about such critical issues as succession of leadership and continuity and preservation of the family legacy and vision.

Ultimately, then, the family council sets policies for the family rather than setting policies for the business, although there is overlap. That said, it can present recommendations to the board around business policies in which the family have an interest or concern. Recommendations are two-way, so the board will emphasise matters around the business which may concern the family and make recommendations on those matters for the family council to consider and provide feedback on.

Vitally, the board of directors and the family council will need to update each other to coordinate concerns, policy decisions and so on. Some family businesses choose to have a family council member sit on the board and a board member sit on the family council as a coordination initiative. Having an annual joint planning session is certainly advisable, as are periodic meetings so that both board and council have a full understanding of what is happening in each forum over the coming twelve months.

Key Activities of the Family Council

The key activities of the family council include:

- Being the key primary link between the family, shareholders, the board and senior management. Maintaining dialogue by communicating regularly and informing the board of directors about the family consensus view regarding policies, strategic plans and innovations in the business.
- Discussing current business, ownership issues, long-term goals and new business ideas and informing the family of same.
- Speaking in one voice by articulating a consensus view, shared vision for the future of the business and its goals, plus a mission statement based on the agreed purpose of the business, along with a set of family values that all family members embrace and that will guide the board, management team and family. Communicating that vision to the family is critical.

- Drafting, revising and finalising the family charter, which includes that vision/mission and purpose along with many other core family policies – such as conflict resolution and conflicts of interest regulation, family members' entry into or exit from the enterprise, and a code of conduct outlining expected behavioural standards of family members. (See the section below for what should be included in the charter or constitution.)
- Helping the family make decisions and reach a consensus around all of these issues.
- Setting up a family office to administer assets and investments that are not related to the business.
- Setting up and overseeing philanthropic initiatives.
- Establishing structures to enable the development and education of younger generations, such as venture funds or scholarships and planning educational programmes.
- Planning and organising meetings, including family assembly meetings, celebrations, leisure activities, social gatherings and other events for family members.
- Distributing a newsletter to the family to inform shareholders and all stakeholders and keep everyone up to speed to enable contribution and build loyalty.
- Deciding how best to develop and prepare the next generation of leaders and managers.
- Acting as gatekeepers to the business to regulate and prevent interference from family members outside of family interaction and involvement policies.
- Ensuring that family goals and targets are met and policies are adhered to.
- Nurturing family members' pride in and commitment to the business through regular communication highlighting consensus decisions made around policies, goals and ownership holdings.

This work by the family council should result in a strengthened system of communication between the family, its staff, shareholders, stakeholders and the management team and board of directors. As such, the family council complements the board of directors perfectly and provides it and management (particularly non-family members of both) with a clear picture around family expectations in terms of how the business is run and where it is headed.

Some advisors suggest that a family council should only be established once the family reaches a critical size, such as more than 30 multigenerational members. Others suggest a family council is necessary regardless of size, as the company and family are both likely to grow. In general, a family council should have fewer than 10 members to simplify its management. Reporting lines must be clearly defined and expectations appropriately managed.

Who Should be on the Family Council?

There are various approaches to deciding who will be part of the family council. If the number of family shareholders and members is relatively small, all family members might become members of the family council. In larger companies, family members will need to be appointed or elected. Ideally, the family council should reflect the family and have a representative cross-section of members. It should have sufficient representation from both genders, every generation from retired to the youngest adult, and include owners who are either actively involved or passively uninvolved, and relatives who are geographically both local and distant.

One of these family council members should be elected as chair and act as the main contact between the council and the family and board of directors. A secretary should also be appointed to take minutes of meetings and distribute them to family members.

Generally, there would be no remuneration packages available for family council members, although expenses may be reimbursed. It typically meets on a quarterly basis, or more frequently if required.

To summarise, the family council acts in a consultative and supportive role. The board of directors of the company initiates, drafts, supports and approves key policies and plans, while the family council is consulted and gives support/feedback on those policies and plans. The only key company document/policy that the family council generates is the family constitution or charter, which focuses on family policy, management and interaction (see below).

2. The Board of Directors

The board of directors focuses solely on the business, establishing strategic direction and policies and steering the business towards achieving its vision and objectives. We will look at the importance of the board, how to choose the right mix of executives and professionalise the business in **Chapter 7**.

As discussed in the last chapter, it is the board of directors that has the responsibility for corporate governance and strategy; the family council governs the family. The board of directors keeps family council members (through the chairman) informed on critical business matters that may affect the family's interests. Members of the board of directors attend board meetings, management meetings and shareholder meetings.

Power is given to the board instead of to individual members, so that it is a depersonalised institution that makes consensus-based decisions and provides a stable structure.

3. The Family Charter or Constitution

While the family council's role is to identify, discuss, decide on and determine all of these policies, issues, etc., the outcome of those deliberations should then be articulated into a family charter.

The family charter or constitution is a statement of principles and purposes, roles and rules, which is recorded and transmitted to all relevant parties, although it is open to change and rewording. It can form the foundation for shareholder unity across multiple generations and decades, and provide a blueprint for the business's success over time.

Family charters are all about clarification – they provide clarity on a number of issues, principles and questions and detail the family's stance on all of these. They also set out how the family and the business interact; outlining the policies that regulate family members' relationships with the business and articulating the guiding vision, mission and values to document the true purpose of the business from the family's point of view.

The key objective, then, is to articulate and draft policies that will guide future actions and decisions across a broad range of areas, for example: resolving conflict and ensuring that ownership rules suit family expectations; setting out how family members should behave in certain situations; which objectives will be laid down for the business; and articulating a variety of family policies and guidelines that will facilitate doing business in an ethical, inclusive and profitable manner.

Benefits of a Family Charter

The key benefit to the business of producing an agreed family charter is that it helps to avoid ending up with more family employees than are needed or, even worse, unsuitable ones. It also supports talent retention by establishing fair employment policies, and can help to avoid conflicts and misunderstandings about who owns what, who does what and why.

For example, let's say some family members who own shares but don't work for the firm wish to gain dividend income; those who do work for the business have opposing interests, wishing to reward those who work for the company and reinvest profits rather than reward non-working shareholders. If you have policies that enable shareholders to liquidate their shares in exchange for cash, that pay out performance-related bonuses before any dividends can be paid and that provide access to company information to all shareholders (i.e. not just those who work for the company), it is then possible to minimise these contentious issues and the potential conflicts that could arise from disparate views, needs and expectations. If everything is clarified early on in this way, everyone knows where they stand. By having a well-informed family council to mull over potentially contentious issues and create appropriate dividend and shareholding policies within the family charter/constitution, it can prevent many headaches down the line.

What Should be Included in a Family Charter?

A family charter or constitution should articulate and include:

- A shared vision for the family business.
- A mission statement.
- The goals and objectives of the family business.
- A statement of core values and principles (for the family members and for the business).
- An employment policy.
- Dividends and family benefits policy.
- Details of the make-up and roles of the family council.
- Details of the family council meetings.

The vision and mission statements should define the purpose and long-term aims of the family business and set out the overall context for determining specific business goals. The Japanese consumer electronics company Sony can provide a good, useful example of effective vision and mission statements.

Sony's vision statement is: "To experience the joy of advancing and applying technology for the benefit of the public"; and its mission statement is: "To become a leading global provider of networked consumer electronics, entertainment and services."

The core values statement should set ethical standards for the business based on the guiding principles of the family as a whole. An example of a core value for a company might be:

"A commitment to sustainability and to acting in an environmentally friendly way."

The family charter (which is a unique document for each family) should also contain details about the role of the family council within the context of governance structures, along with rules about how the family will govern itself and interact with corporate bodies, such as the board of directors.

A list of topics that might be addressed and headings that could be included in any family constitution is set out in **Appendix 6.2** to this chapter. For our present purposes, general matters that need to be considered when drafting a family charter include:

1. General considerations.
2. The board and the executive management team (a description of the make-up of both and how they will interact).
3. Family member employment guidelines.
4. Ownership guidelines and policy.
5. A family code of conduct (which sets out the desired behaviour of the family towards other family members and employees).
6. Other family policies.
7. A communication policy and information-sharing guidelines.

We will now examine issues under each of these headings in more detail. As no two family businesses are the same, the remainder of this chapter will present a variety of questions to be addressed, leaving it to the reader to decide which are relevant for his or her own family business.

This is a comprehensive guide, from which each reader can take those elements particularly relevant to his or her business. By doing this, you can create a template for the family governance structures required by your business, and proceed accordingly.

1. General Considerations

QUESTIONS TO CONSIDER IN DRAFTING A FAMILY CHARTER

- Why does the family want to be in business together?

- What is the shared vision for the future of the business? What is the family's mission and purpose for the business? Where do you see the business in five, 10, 30 years? What are the key family objectives and goals for the business over the coming few years? The answers to these questions will form the basis of the family vision and mission statements, as well as the business vision and mission statement.

- What are the family's core values and principles that should guide the business and be reflected in the way the business is run?

- What are the key drivers that got the family and the business to where they are now?

- What are family members' expectations over the long term? What returns are the family members looking for?

- How relevant is the family's history/heritage to its vision, mission and purpose?

- What is the role of the business in supporting *family* goals?

- What are the main priorities for the family going forward? Is it to preserve family control over the business and create a legacy for future generations? Is it to grow capital, retain earnings and sell the business in years to come? Is it to have the best management team running the business, regardless of whether or not they are family members? Strategically, is it preferable for the family to be working for the business or the business to be working for the family, or both? How so? Examine these priorities.

2. *The Board and the Executive Management Team*

QUESTIONS TO CONSIDER IN DRAFTING A FAMILY CHARTER

- How important is it for family members to hold the position of chairman or CEO and make up the executive management team and/or board of directors? Should the family be led by an external expert/professional or a family member? Who should appoint this leader and make the decision about that appointment?

- What rules should there be about who can be on the board and work in the business?

- How will the board be composed and what will its role be?

- How should the board be comprised in order to get the right mix and ensure that the board is balanced (i.e. with sufficient input from outside the business and the family)?

- How will the family participate in director selection?

- How will board members be selected and appraised?

- What will be the role of non-executive directors?

- How will the board and owners/shareholders communicate?

- Which decisions shall be reserved primarily for the board?

- How much power is given to the board? A board of directors' policy which clarifies the role, responsibilities and powers of the board of directors needs to be documented.

3. *Family Member Employment Guidelines*

QUESTIONS TO CONSIDER IN DRAFTING A FAMILY CHARTER

- Should senior management positions be reserved for family members? How might that negatively impact the motivation of non-family managers who may feel that they will never be senior management, regardless of how hard they work? What talent attraction and retention consequences might result from such a policy?

- How can you ensure your employment policy is fair in order to motivate all and attract/retain the best family and non-family management/executives?

- What guidelines will you put in place to provide an objective basis for deciding which family members should be eligible to join the family business? Or, is a role in the family business a birthright for all family members, regardless of ability/experience?

- What must family members be able to contribute to the business in order to be eligible? What are the criteria for entry? What age, educational qualifications, skills, experience/competence level should be required from family members to join the business as an employee and enhance that level of contribution? (For example, should younger generations get outside experience prior to joining the family firm? If so, for how long? Two to five years, including a promotion? What might the benefits of that be? A stronger sense of commitment over the long term and not viewing the company as an entitlement or a fail-safe security blanket?)

- How will family staff members be managed? For example, by non-family managers to enable objective appraisal and unbiased feedback?

- How will you ensure that all family members receive fair, competitive compensation and are held accountable to certain standards of performance?

- What career development policies and opportunities might be provided for the next generation and in-laws?

- What if a family member fails to perform adequately? How might firing a family member impact on the family?

- How can non-family employees best be motivated?

- How will you engage the younger generation to join and stay with the family firm?

- How do you choose between siblings or cousins to fill a role without showing favouritism?

- How will you decide on the next manager/leader of the business and choose between siblings/cousins? Would non-family members be considered for the CEO role?

- How do you ensure that family members who are not employed in the business are treated fairly?

4. Ownership Guidelines and Policy

The ownership and transfer of shares and the rights, roles and responsibilities of shareholders need to be documented. This should include:

- A definition of rights, roles, responsibilities, expectations and obligations of all shareholders (everyone who owns shares in the business).
- Clarity around the rights and roles of those individuals that could lead to uncertainty in the future (such as in-laws, spouses and so on).
- A shareholder agreement that outlines which kinds of decision might be made by owners as opposed to the board, how shares might be valued and rules regarding the transfer and ownership of shares, plus principles governing shareholder liquidity and capital allocation, including company loans and share redemption, appropriate dividend and reinvestment levels. (For example, some shareholders may prefer to sell shares for cash, particularly minority shareholders, when the shareholder pool grows and shares are diluted, resulting in lower dividends. The shareholder agreement should provide clarity around mechanisms to sell shares providing liquidity options via a shares redemption fund, e.g. financed by a small percentage of profits, to buy back family members' liquidated shares.)
- An ownership/management succession policy and plan/ framework that sets the guidelines and expectations around ownership/leadership/management succession. (See **Chapter 10** on succession.)

QUESTIONS TO CONSIDER IN DRAFTING A FAMILY CHARTER

- Who should be allowed to own shares and why? Should they only be held by family members? If so, which kind of family member? For example, bloodline descendants of the founder only, or in-laws (spouses/partners) also? Does diversity strengthen or dilute ownership? Is it important to have, for instance, both parents (spouses therefore included) as shareholders to help convey a positive message regarding the family enterprise? Or is it more important to have a smaller ownership group with a shared understanding and vision, such as bloodline family members, to prevent complications that could occur if marriages fail?

- If only family members should own shares, how will you incentivise non-family members/executives (who don't own shares)? For example, might different classes of share be established, such as voting rights for family members and non-voting shares for non-family members? Or could non-family shareholders hold shares in a subsidiary company rather than the holding company?

- How will share ownership be transferred from one generation to the next?

- Which shares are matrimonial property? (Matrimonial property essentially means that all matrimonial property could be divided equally between the spouses when a marriage ends (depending on the law of the land).) What can be done to avoid them being matrimonial property (e.g. gifted shares from a non-spouse, inherited or acquired before marriage and not bought)?

- Should potential spouses of shareholders sign prenuptial agreements?

- How should shares/control be divided among family members?

- What rules should be put in place around share transference and ownership to protect the business from shares being sold or transferred inappropriately? Will there be pre-emption rights, for example, to enable existing family shareholders to retain shares in the family business?

- How should shareholders be compensated? How can shareholders' expectations be aligned with the business growth/exit strategy? What dividend strategy/stock redemption mechanism should be put in place to enable fair compensation?

- What formal provision for liquidity options/share buy-back arrangements should be put in place to provide minority shareholders with the chance to liquidate shares for cash?

- Will a shares redemption fund be financed by a small percentage of profits, in order to buy back family members' liquidated shares?

- How much participation in the business should be expected from shareholders and non-shareholders?

- How can balance be achieved between custodian shareholders (who opt for reinvestment of profits for future gains) and value-out shareholders (who prefer to get the best return on investment now)? How will you ensure that your dividend policy addresses the interests of family shareholders and the business's growth?

- Should performance-related bonuses be paid before dividends to reward those in the company (family and non-family) who deliver the most value?

- How can conflict between working owners and non-working owners be avoided/minimised? For instance, through clarity of dividend policy and remuneration policy for working owners and decision-making policies regarding working and non-working participation and expectation? By having these policies in place, both forms of owners understand their financial return.

- Who can be included in the decision-making process regarding reinvestment/distribution of profits?

- How can family ownership of shares be sustained? How critical is that?

- What are the principles of ownership succession? How will the family groom and appoint the best successor? What will the role of the family be in ownership and management succession? (For a detailed examination of the matters and consequences surrounding succession, see **Chapter 10**.)

5. *A Family Code of Conduct*

QUESTIONS TO CONSIDER IN DRAFTING A FAMILY CHARTER

- As a family, how do you wish to be seen by non-family members/employees/the general public?

- What traits and characteristics do you wish to display as a family unit?

- How will your family values inform your code of conduct?

- How should you treat each other in the workplace and outside of it?

- How do you wish to be represented at management/board level?

6. *Other Family Policies*

POLICIES TO CONSIDER IN DRAFTING A FAMILY CHARTER

- A conflict resolution policy, which outlines actions to take and processes to follow in the event of a conflict between family members or between members of the family and the board. The objective of this policy is to resolve such conflict and balance stakeholder interests to avoid jeopardising the continuity of the family business.

- A decision-making policy, which defines methods and sets a clear framework for decision making that aims to get the right balance between making business decisions for family reasons, and family decisions for business reasons.

- A PR policy, which provides guidelines for publicity and the family/business's role within the wider community, defines the family as a brand, and so on.

- An education policy, which sets out how the family and next generation will be educated and developed.

- A philanthropic policy, which sets out guidelines for philanthropic, civic and charitable activities, and the administration, coordination and funding of shared interests.

- Financial planning and estate planning policies, including the development of a retirement and personal financial plan for business leaders that also determines risk and the value of corporate investment and asset portfolios.

7. Communication Policy and Information-sharing Guidelines

QUESTIONS TO CONSIDER IN DRAFTING A FAMILY CHARTER

- How will information be shared among the family and how will good family communication be fostered? Through which channels and how frequently will this be done?

- How will education be encouraged? How will the younger generation be educated about the business and family heritage, vision and traditions?

- How will family members be able to develop their skills and be prepared for leadership?

- How will family values, principles and vision be passed on to the younger generation?
- How will family archives be maintained and family history be celebrated?

This examination of the various facets of a family charter should have made clear the extent of the issues to be considered and discussed, and also the fact that there is no 'one size fits all' solution to family governance – all families and all enterprises are different. Family governance institutions and constitutions should be tailor-made for each business, depending on how involved family members are and wish to be, what the family dynamics are like, and how big, old and complex the family business is.

Hopefully, what has also become clear from this discussion is the absolute necessity of, and huge benefits to be derived from compiling a charter that is comprehensive, well-thought-out and has the support of family, board and shareholders. It can be an essential tool in creating a sound foundation for the business and its future.

In the next chapter, we will follow on from the best practice guidelines on corporate and family governance by examining how to professionalise the family business. This entails, at its base, inviting and incorporating external, independent directors onto the board. This can be a big step for a family business used to operating as a 'closed shop', but it is an important, and often a hugely beneficial step for a family business to take if profitability and sustainability are to be top of the agenda.

Appendix 6.1: Questionnaire for Individual Family Members

The following is a questionnaire to be distributed to all family members at the time of drafting a family charter. The purpose of the exercise is to get an understanding of the individual family members' views and achieve a balance of views in the charter.

QUESTIONNAIRE FOR FAMILY MEMBERS

- What are you passionate about?
- What is your true purpose in life?
- What activities have you undertaken in order to pursue that passionate purpose?
- How do you achieve balance between work, family and leisure?
- What are your roles within the family enterprise?
- How has the family business helped you to achieve your personal goals and aspirations?
- How has your family helped you to achieve your personal goals and aspirations?
- What roles do you hope to have in the future?
- What are your expectations for yourself in terms of ambition within or outside the family firm?
- How would you hope to be remembered?
- What have you given to yourself, your family, your community?
- What kind of family do you have?
- What are the core values and guiding principles that guide the family?
- What are the core values and guiding principles that guide the family business?

- What has led your family business to be successful thus far?

- How would others describe your family?

- What is your own personal vision for the business?

- What is the mission of the family business?

- Where do you hope to see the family business in 5–10 years' time?

- Are you and other family members committed to the business? How so?

- How are the core values and guiding principles passed on to the next generation?

- How will you pass those values and principles on?

- How does the family take care of its older, retiring or retired members?

- How does the family look after, educate and engage its younger members?

- How is development nurtured?

- How is conflict managed and resolved?

- How are expectations communicated?

- How often does the family get together socially?

- Who leads the business and what key qualities do they have?

- What leadership qualities do you feel the management team should have?

- Are there any gaps in skills/knowledge/expertise/qualities that need to be filled?

- Is there a succession plan?

- What are your views on succession? Who should be the successor and why?

- How influential are older members of the family in the business?

- How influential are younger members of the family in the business?

- What might you do differently to optimise inclusion for all?

- How is leadership performance monitored and held accountable?

- Is there a family council? Should there be?

- Would you like to be a member of the council? Why?

- How are stakeholder interests aligned and balanced?

Appendix 6.2: Suggested Structure for a Family Constitution

PART A: INTRODUCTION

PART B: THE FAMILY CODE OF ETHICS

B.1 Overview
B.2 Aim
B.3 Shared Values
B.4 Personal Code of Conduct

PART C: STRUCTURE

C.1 Definitions
C.2 The Legal and Practical Structures
C.3 Amendment of the Family Constitution

PART D: OWNERSHIP OF THE BUSINESS

D.1 Ownership and voting control
D.2 Transfers of Shares and Pre-emption Rights
D.3 Share Valuation
D.4 Exit Routes
D.5 Outside Interests
D.6 Confidentiality
D.7 Communication
D.8 Family Council

PART E: OPERATION AND MANAGEMENT OF THE BUSINESS

E.1 Objectives and Management Philosophy
E.2 Leadership
E.3 Group Board of directors
E.4. Family Jobs and Remuneration
E.5. Dividends
E.6 Employees

PART F: THE NEXT GENERATION

F.1 Introduction
F.2 Summer Jobs
F.3 Permanent Jobs
F.4 Satellite Ventures

CHAPTER 7

Bringing in the Right Expertise: Professionalising the Business

Introduction

Statistics reveal that at least 35% of Fortune 500 companies are family-controlled.[1] All of these family firms were, at some point, much smaller enterprises that kept things in the family during the early stages. But one day, each of those family firms took the plunge to become more professional and more rigorous in order to compete on the international stage, where risks and rewards are far greater.

When family businesses grow, owners have to adapt their management styles to the demands of a larger, more complex business. For any family firm to continue to grow, the instinctive management styles of the founders must give way to a more professional approach to business, which means appointing a board of directors.

There comes a point in the lifecycle of all companies when they outgrow their foundational framework and need to recruit external, non-family board members. Such key senior figures should be a catalyst for growth and, as such, their designation is likely to have a crucial impact on the success of a company. Recruiting at this level enables the owner/manager to step back from the day-to-day running of the business and take it to the next level with guidance from an official support network of trusted advisors and experts. Additionally, having a board in place and knowing that, as CEO, you need to report to it about what's going on in the business encourages a longer-term focus and more disciplined mindset.

[1] Bernard, C., "Family Control in Business" (8 August 2013) www.kpmgfamilybusiness.com/family-control-in-business.

What Does it Mean to 'Professionalise'?

Family businesses tend to start out small, but as they grow, so too must their systems and the owners need to adapt their management style to the demands of a larger, more complex business if they are to survive and thrive. The management methods used must therefore give way to a more professionalised approach based on established management techniques.

Professionalising a family business that has traditionally been a relatively informal operation can be challenging, not just because of the work involved in formalising governance and management practices, recruiting board members and the process of holding management accountable, but because there can be resistance from family members to recruiting outsiders to take up such important and influential positions in the company.

Fears and misconceptions about confidentiality, control and respect can surface, or the family may feel that the skills required at board level already exist in-house. Sometimes it can be difficult to find someone suitable who is willing to take up a position on the board. Despite all of these excuses for continuing to 'keep it in the family', there comes a time when recruiting some external board members is a necessary ingredient to sustainable growth and making the business more professional in its operation. The key question to ask here is: do you want to be a **family** business or a family **business**?

Why Professionalise?

Professionalising the business by engaging external board members is an important step in the evolution of a family firm as it grows beyond a point where the family can effectively manage it. An independent board of directors, which complements the positive dynamics of the family enterprise, is an enormously valuable resource and a proven part of the management systems used by the world's most successful companies. Professionalisation gives the family business the best chance of survival, from the first generation to third and fourth and beyond. As such, you owe it to the business, as a family, to ensure not just good ownership, but good management too. Indeed, independent boards with the requisite skills and experience together with family stakeholders can create a powerful and formidable alliance with faster revenue growth thanks to more deliberate and disciplined strategic practices and processes.

The role of director should not belong exclusively to family members because it is empowering for the business if the family members leading it work alongside a majority (or at least significant minority) of experienced and qualified independent directors. This will provide an extra layer of support and skills to help deal with the increasing complexity of a growing family firm. Directors brought in from outside the family can act as a helpful sounding board in providing advice and counsel to the business owners, leaders and key management.

At some point on its journey from being a start-up, a family business will be in danger of losing its competitive advantage. Over time, uniqueness and commitment can diminish while succession and other family-related issues can increase the complexity of management. To take the business through its life cycles it needs to be very well managed. That's where the board of directors comes in. Shared decision-making responsibility and the controlled, planned growth that comes from having a board of directors with external members on it frees up the family-business owner to focus on providing leadership and vision. The board enables that vision to come to fruition through providing money, facilities and people at the right time; it also helps shareholders reach a consensus and make the right decisions to enable sustainable growth.

As the company develops, additional skills may be required to support the strategy; for example, the company may be looking to expand into a different country or acquire certain types of companies. The appointment of a non-executive director (NED) with these particular skills to the board can help achieve the company's strategy.

The Benefits of Introducing Independent Directors

The benefits of professionalising the business with a partially or wholly independent board are many, and include:

- Gaining a fresh external perspective and accessing experience and skills that the business may not otherwise have had.

- Replacing confusion and complexity with a logical organisational structure and regular meetings with well-organised and managed agendas.
- Empowering growth and performance as a result of formalising long-term strategic plans, monitoring implementation of those plans and holding annual business reviews, among other board-related initiatives.
- Being better equipped to respond to family shareholders' concerns around strategy, objectives, policies, etc.
- Improving the objectivity and quality of decision making that affects the business (planning and creative thinking) and the family members (such as evaluating performance, determining compensation, hiring and terminating family members, identifying successors, and better managing expectations and conflicts).
- Promoting continuity and stability by mentoring and supporting successors, and providing departing generations with peace of mind.
- Improving discipline and governance as the management are held accountable by the board and the board ensures that the business operates within a strict set of rules. Gaining improved credibility by showing stakeholders that your family firm means business.
- Further improving credibility by showing that there is no favouritism towards family members. (Non-family board members and senior managers can establish governance measures for discouraging nepotism, such as setting merit-based criteria for family member recruitment.)
- Reducing owner dependency. The board empowers the business by creating and implementing an infrastructure and policies that move beyond such dependency.
- Enabling better benchmarking against industry, national or global best practice.
- Enhancing strategic alliances and other cooperative and collaborative relationships with suppliers, customers, employees and the community.
- Providing new ambassadors for the business.

The Consequences of *Not* Having Independent Directors

Reluctance in bringing in external directors can be very detrimental to a family firm. It can lead to lack of delegation, foresight, innovation or ability to move with the times, along with an incessant need to keep the company's money within the family to satisfy its material requirements or fund its lifestyle. All of these issues stunt business growth (which has the knock-on effect of limiting the financial health of future generations).

Ultimately, the board is the company's steering group. Having a blend of executive and non-executive directors (NEDs) as a company grows will add the additional skills that may be required to support the strategy of the company, for example if the company was looking to expand into a new market or acquire a competing business. The appointment of an NED with these particular skills can help the board achieve the company's strategy.

The role of an NED is to provide objective, independent advice to the board. They should add value through their high-calibre status, wealth of external wisdom and experience, and high-level connections. **They help family businesses to focus on the business of business**. After all, the decision-making process for the family in business can sometimes be too closed, with creative and fresh thinking occasionally lost in the tangled web of familial relationships and expectations. Guidance from advisors and board members who are not affiliated with family members can provide the business with an effective 'reality check'.

Composition of the Board of Directors

Chairman **Board of Directors and Chief Executive/Managing Director** **Management Team**

The board should generally be chaired by an independent non-executive chairman (NEC). The appointment of a NEC is an important step in shaping the corporate governance of a company. A chairperson brings experience, increased profile and a more rigorous approach to corporate governance. The chairperson usually sets the agenda, schedules meetings and coordinates actions of subcommittees within the board.

In terms of the organisation and the three main stakeholders, the senior management represents the employees, whereas the family council is the voice of the family, while the board of directors is the voice and organising mechanism of the family business owners and work on the business for the good of the business. This enables those 'three circles' (discussed in **Chapter 5**) within the family business system to work together effectively.

Making the transition from the de facto board of 'founder and spouse' or simply 'family members' to establishing an independent board of directors is huge step for any family business in securing long-term success. The decision to establish a formal board of directors is the most significant step in the development of the corporate governance framework for a family business, and indeed for most businesses in general.

While there are many very successful companies that do not have a formal board, in general the appointment of a board with the appropriate skills and expertise will be of enormous benefit to an ambitious company. The appointment of a board means there will be a greater degree of formality in place, and this is likely to result in greater attention to detail and better decision-making processes. The responsibilities of the board are separate and distinct from those of management; the board does not manage the company.

The following questions should be considered if the business is ready for this move:

- Is the managing director/founder committed to making the concept of an independent board work?
- Is the business a growing, maturing company?
- Is the business substantial enough that the shareholder and operation issues can be distinguished from one another?
- Will non-executive directors enhance the board and add to the existing professional advisers that the company uses?

The stewardship of the company by the MD/founder will be under scrutiny when an independent board is appointed and this is something that he or she will have to cope with, as in the past they are likely to have made all the decisions.

Smaller boards, with between five and eight members (but without family member domination), tend to work best for family businesses. Board effectiveness is strongly influenced by the number and the qualifications of board members. Ideally, the board should include the chief executive/MD, external independent board members (non-family/non-management) that are non-executive, along with a small group of family representatives who may or may not be shareholders or management. To ensure that board members remain engaged and also to avoid any one member over-influencing or even intimidating the rest, the board ideally needs to have a dynamic composition of executive and non-executive directors bringing different skill sets to the board.

Friends, family members not involved in the business and advisors to the family (such as lawyers, accountants or bankers) should not be invited to sit on the board. While key senior management (management team executives) may be invited to join the board, operational company managers should not be included as there is a tendency for them to focus on operational issues rather than issues of strategy. It can also make evaluating the quality of company management more difficult if one of the managers is part of that discussion process. Of course, company managers can be invited to participate in the occasional meeting and it is likely that key members of the management team, such as the chief executive and finance director, will be on the board. If a manager is invited to attend a board meeting, it is up to the board to decide in advance how long that person will remain in the meeting, to enable board members to talk freely without that person present.

Above all, boards must be independent and act solely in the interest of the business. Furthermore, the board members must be free from any conflicts that could compromise their judgment.

How Board Members are Appointed

Shareholders generally elect and appoint the board of directors, which may include some members of the senior management team. Only those family members who occupy senior positions in the business or who are designated to be successors to senior positions in the very near future (i.e. close to assuming a leadership role), should be invited to join the board. Otherwise there can be confusion as to who reports to whom. It is wise to allow the family council and/or shareholders to select the family representatives who are likely to be the most valuable and representative family members on the board.

The family charter or constitution usually addresses how board members are appointed. Some considerations are as follows:

- Who can serve?
- How is that determined and by whom?
- Should board members be compensated?
- How will the board interact with the family?
- How is the board structured and what are its commitments and responsibilities?

See **Appendix 7.1** for a helpful flowchart detailing the key steps and considerations necessary when appointing authorities to the board.

Board Meetings

Board meetings should be held as frequently and for as long as it takes to ensure meaningful engagement takes places. An 'away day' to plan the following year's activities and discuss strategy and performance can be a very good practice. Board members may also work in between meetings on various assignments and to prepare for the next board meeting.

It is good practice to have lunch or dinner after a board meeting, as this provides a good opportunity to build relationships among board members, who may not otherwise meet in an informal setting.

The quorum (the minimum number of directors required) for board meetings can be fixed by directors (according to the Companies Act 1963 (as amended), Schedule 1, Table A, Part I, regulation 102) and unless it is so fixed, two directors satisfy the quorum for business to be validly transacted. Matters are decided at board meetings on the basis of a majority of votes cast; the chairperson can exercise a second and deciding vote if there is deadlock and an equal number of votes for and against are cast by the directors (Companies Act 1963 (as amended), Schedule 1, Table A, Part I, regulation 101).

(Table A sets out the model regulations within the Companies Acts. These regulations are relevant to private limited companies and are typically what the articles of association are based on. The regulations of Table A are then applied, disapplied or modified within the articles of association depending on the needs of the company.)

The Role of the Board

Boards consist of executive and non-executive directors (NEDs). Essentially, while the board manages the company and takes decisions on behalf of the company, the senior management team manages the business and implements board decisions. In order for the board to make informed decisions, it relies heavily on materials prepared by management. So, in general, **while the board works *on* the business, the management team work *in* the business**.

The role of the board is to hold the management team to account and to protect the interests of shareholders, which is why the entire executive management team should not be on the board (only key members should be). The board must support the lead director and oversee the high-level affairs of the company to ensure stability, sustainability and growth. Some companies choose instead to furnish the board exclusively with NEDs to make it easier to hold the management team accountable and assess their performance.

Essentially, the role of the board is to:

- represent and protect the interests of the shareholders;
- monitor and review the performance of the company (oversight);
- provide leadership of the company (advisory); and
- consult with management regarding the strategic and operational direction of the company.

The Role of the Chairman and Other Non-executive Directors

Following best practice in corporate governance, the chairman is quite likely to be an NED. It is his or her role to manage the board and advise on direction and strategy to help the business to grow.

As well as managing the board itself, the chairman should also manage board meetings and their agendas. The chairman can be invaluable in acting as the glue to hold a company and its strategic vision together. As the main board members (i.e. chairman, chief executive/MD, chief operating officer (COO) and chief financial officer (CFO)) form the spine of the team, they must be aligned in terms of the mission and vision of the firm and know where the company is heading. If they are not adequately aligned, they will find it difficult not only to spearhead and guide the company but also to adhere to their wider obligations. In fact, the new Companies Bill in Ireland clearly states that the job of both the chief executive and the chairman is to act in the interests of all stakeholders, not just shareholders.

The role of chairman tends to be a blend of advisor, adjudicator, regulator and mentor. The chairman and other NEDs on the board should also exhibit a good mix of challenge and mentoring. They will encourage, coach and advise while also questioning and challenging the consensus. Typically, NEDs will guide the company through the various stages of growth and help to professionalise the company. Depending on their realm of expertise, they can assist with planning the business structure, building the management team, creating/reviewing budgets and providing astute commercial contacts and a more mature approach to finances, planning and strategic alliances.

Non-executive directors provide a new dimension of objectivity and wealth of experience to the board. A good NED can help build consensus between family shareholders and board members. Good NEDs are typically self-confident team players without ego issues who can provide an impartial view on issues such as management, succession, employment, compensation, and can contribute confidently to strategic debate.

The Role of the Executive Management Team

Behind every great chief executive/MD there is a great executive management team to manage the business (operations director, financial director, sales and marketing director, HR director, etc.). As stated above, key members of the executive management team will often sit on the board.

Essentially, the role of the executive management team is to manage the business on a day-to-day operational level. It is their responsibility to monitor the performance of staff and ensure they are adhering to the strategy. While the board should ensure that the executive management team is prepared for any contingencies or market shifts, so the executive management team must adequately prepare all staff for such issues.

The management team must drive revenue and deliver; they must also help the teams they manage to do the same. They need to have a detailed knowledge of each area of the business so they can see the bigger picture. They need a wealth of experience and expertise within the trade, plus strong business acumen.

The executive management team must also ensure they meet employment regulations while effectively motivating and managing staff. As direct reports to the chief executive/MD, members of the executive management team must also communicate regularly to the CEO, who must communicate regularly with the board.

As such, when it comes to recruiting members of both the board of directors and the executive management team, certain skills are imperative. For example, CEOs often display great creative and business development skills, while managers and CFOs have meticulous attention to detail. They need to be operationally organised and efficient, and skilled at prioritising. Each 'type' of contribution must be well managed if the contribution of that person is to be maximised.

Responsibilities of the Board

Each board member will bring different experiences and skills to the table, but all will share the primary duties and responsibilities of the board. Boards are not only about governance, they are also about adding value. Those who sit on a board should help to increase the capital value of a business through their collective wisdom, experience, knowledge and contacts in order to ultimately help the company flourish. It is the responsibility of every board member to:

- monitor the performance and liquidity of the business;
- monitor the quality and capability of the executive management team and their performance in implementing and executing strategy, and provide feedback on same to the chief executive/executive management team;

- supervise the recruitment of new members of the executive management team, including succession planning;
- regularly appraise the sustainability of the business model;
- help set and/or support the strategy (or flag concerns) about the direction of the business;
- establish and communicate the values and vision of the business;
- evaluate and identify threats, weaknesses, strengths and opportunities of the family business;
- protect the interests of the shareholders and the company and oversee the family's involvement in the business, communicating regularly and effectively with the chair of the family council (who may also sit on the board); and
- develop policies that complement those laid out in the family charter or constitution and enable the company and shareholders to achieve their goals.

One of the responsibilities listed above is to protect shareholders' interests, which is a primary duty of each and every board member. It is important, however, for board members to balance their commitments between shareholders' needs and those of the company. For instance, paying out large dividends to shareholders may suit the shareholders, but it may not align with the goals or needs of the business. Carrying out such actions could weaken the business and reduce shareholder value over the long term. As such, balancing the company needs and those of the shareholders is a vital requirement for board members and can be tricky to manage; hence the need for experience and expertise in dealing with such matters.

Independent board members and those who are family members must equally understand the family's objectives, relationships and politics. They may need to mediate the family's involvement and influence to ensure that the family's needs around finance and employment do not harm the long-term viability of the company. This will probably mean that some time should be devoted to outlining these issues. However, family issues should be managed by the family council to free up the board as much as possible to focus on the running of the company.

Boards without any independent directors, where the board members are all family members, can find it difficult to consider longer-term viability issues as their vision and experience maybe limited to the family business only and they may lack the years of diverse experience that non-executive directors can bring to a business. That is where an independent board is useful, as it is able to advise on strategy, vision, growth plans, development of financial and human relationships, succession, strategic alliances and the ability to compete. This is important because it is the responsibility of the board to plan out the short, medium and long-term goals of the business and to work to achieve those goals in a timely and cost-effective manner.

Ideally, the board should be proactive rather than reactive – it should not only have a firm grasp of the core strategy and model but also have a good knowledge of the key performance indicators ('KPIs', or the agreed quantifiable measurements that demonstrate the success of a business), overall operating costs and market position so that they can flag up and advise on potential threats or opportunities relating to performance.

As such, it is the responsibility of each board member to be aware of the overall health of the company – not only the financial indicators but customer satisfaction and employee engagement as well. While management may set certain policies and the family council may set family-related ones, the board of directors sets the main key policies or, at the very least, sets policies that impact the company overall and ensure consistency of performance. For instance, the family council may draft a policy about hiring family members, which would then be reviewed by the board, with recommended amendments noted. The board would then approve and enforce the policy.

While the ideal is to find high-calibre, experienced board members from outside the company, it is important to remember that, if they have a blue-chip corporate mindset, they will need to be able to adapt and empathise with the outlook of a small and growing business, its resources and culture. If they cannot, they may demand reporting or analysis that smaller businesses cannot stretch to, or they may lack the flexibility or fast-paced decision making that smaller businesses require. The right blend of backgrounds and approaches is therefore vital.

How Does a Family Business Professionalise Effectively?

Having examined the outcomes of professionalising the family business, we must now consider how this process can be effectively planned and implemented. It is important to plan very carefully for the process of professionalising the business, ensuring that all relevant parties understand the reasoning behind this move, how it will be enacted and the target outcomes and benefits for the company. This means lots of information and communication circulating among management and staff before embarking on this process.

Fortunately, the structural and organisational changes required to professionalise the board are relatively straightforward, especially if a family council and constitution are already in place:

1. Shifting the family mindset to embrace independent directors.
2. Having a committed executive management team.
3. Appointing the best directors.

1. Shifting the Family Mindset to Embrace Independent Directors

It is important to stress that professionalising the business does not mean removing family members from management and leadership roles, leaving external executives to run the firm in a strictly conventional way. There is still much to be said for the entrepreneurial spirit that founders have and that family businesses often embrace as part of their culture. However, balance is imperative for sustainable success in business and that goes for the make-up of the top tier of leaders as well. So rather than minimising the family's role in running the company, the ideal way to professionalise a business is to manage the interface between the family and the business and enable sustainable growth by bringing in some external independent executives as board members, while also retaining some family leaders and shareholders as board members (and management team executives).

It is important to educate all shareholders and stakeholders about the positive impact professionalising the business will have. Clarifying accountabilities, responsibilities and roles of family members, improving governance and vital strategic planning as the business develops and grows in complexity and size are all winning factors. As long as any detractors can be persuaded that family participation, control or influence will not be adversely affected and that the family's core values and culture will not change, then the process should move along without resentment or suspicion among staff or family members.

CASE STUDY: OFFICE CLEANING SERVICES – THE POSITIVE IMPACT OF PROFESSIONALISING[2]

Office Cleaning Services (OCS) was founded in 1930 by Frederick Goodliffe. His great-grandson, Chris Cracknell, now runs the firm, having joined in 1977. The family enterprise employs 76,000 people, including 26,000 in the UK. It is one of the largest privately owned companies in Britain, with a turnover of £800 million.

OCS has 130 individual shareholders, of which all but five are members of the original founding family. After intense diversification by Goodliffe's three sons, the board was family-based until the late 1980s, when it sold some of those diversified businesses to focus on support services and to embrace globalisation. (It has succeeded in doing so, and is now the second largest British-owned employer in Thailand, with 26,000 staff there.)

In order to manage those transitions – of succession, selling parts of the firm and embracing globalisation – the family's traditional control needed to be loosened and the business professionalised with the inclusion of external non-executive directors. The first of these were appointed in 1999, while five years later a share option scheme for senior management was introduced. OCS now also has remuneration, nominations and audit committees with external non-executive directors, including a group chairman.

Chris Cracknell believes the group has progressed from being family-owned and run to being family-owned and professionally managed: "We're now a meritocracy and the board is not just reserved for the family. It's helped preserve our family culture, ethics, background and style as an organisation. I think it's a differentiator that's enabled us to compete and grow to the size we are today.

---

[2] Cave, A., "Family firms defy downturn as generation game fuels profits", *The Telegraph*, 2 March 2013.

"The key stage was a recognition that the family relied very heavily on the board management team and staff who worked in the group to make it successful and go forward.

"Secondly, there was a recognition by the family that there was no genetic predisposition that they had the capability to run it and that we needed expertise to come in. My successor could be family or non-family. At the end of the day, all of our interests are best served by having the best people to lead us in the future."[3]

2. Having a Committed Executive Management Team

The executive management team should be committed and motivated to enable the process to work, and clear communication should take place between management and the owners/shareholders every step of the way. First, expectations should be determined and the priorities, needs and objectives of key family members addressed by the management team. The points where family and business overlap should be understood and addressed as part of the overall professionalisation process, so that everyone is sure of where they stand.

3. Appointing the Best Directors

My advice is to appoint the best directors the company can afford (see below for a discussion on how to find directors who are the best fit for the company). Prepare information for potential directors to read in order to familiarise themselves with the scope and intent of the business. This prospectus might include the current business plan, formal control systems, operational procedures and management processes, and the family charter or constitution (see **Chapter 6**). It is the chairman of the board that approaches potential directors on behalf of the company. The chairman of the board needs to be able to clearly communicate the vision, mission, values and strategic objectives of the firm, its strengths and weaknesses, and its position within the marketplace. The chairman must also be able to pinpoint issues that the board could focus on to develop the existing foundations and enable growth.

[3] *Ibid.*

How to Choose the Right Directors for the Board

Once the family business has taken the decision to professionalise, it must then identify directors and executive management team members with the right skills and expertise and invite them to join the board. In appointing the best people to help guide the company towards growth and achieve shareholders' aspirations, it is important to understand the roles each board member will perform and the ideal skills, qualities and attitudes they should exhibit to suit the needs of the business (see below).

The first vital task is to analyse the gap between where the company is now and where it wishes to be in order to clearly define what (and who) is needed to achieve those ambitions. Strong board directors will bring a wealth of experience and proven good judgement, independent thinking, inquisitiveness and a well-rounded knowledge of the industry and, if possible, the firm itself and its business culture (although the latter can be learned).

While the attitudes and perspectives of the board should range along a wide scale between dreamers/believers and cynics/challengers, a wide knowledge and competency base is also crucial. Expertise and experience are probably the most desirable qualities for a board member to have and are essential when it comes to leadership.

What Skills are Needed on the Board?

It is the expertise quotient that makes having non-executive directors (NEDs) on the board so attractive to growing businesses. Understanding the core drivers of your company's growth will help you determine the specific competencies that you would benefit from the most. You need the right blend of skills at the right time.

In assessing the skills and experience your family business needs on its board and among its management team, start by considering the following:

- What are your aspirations for the business? Base the initial recruitment and ongoing evaluation of the board (and, indeed, the executive management team) one step ahead of the firm's current position so that their competencies relate directly to the target growth.

- What is the optimal skills portfolio you need to have at the board table, based on your growth strategy?
- What are the existing skills of board members, and what's missing? Always strive to identify knowledge gaps quickly so they can be addressed effectively, and continually question what skills are missing to achieve the company's goals. Ensure that every new recruit to the board complements, rather than simply duplicates, existing expertise.

Leadership Qualities Checklist for the Board and Management Team

Directors plan the direction the company will take; managers manage the implementation of that strategic direction. Ultimately, to fulfil both of these roles there are certain additional requirements that go beyond general attitudes and realms of expertise.

As well as being skilled experts with industry experience and connections, good management team and board members should also possess sound leadership skills. This is a tougher demand than it may seem, because sound leadership skills are difficult to acquire and master. All too often directors are founts of knowledge when it comes to their expert topic, but when it comes to leading people, they can fail. Whether running a start-up or a 100-strong team, there are some common attributes that all company leaders should possess.

According to research carried out by the Directorbank Group (a UK market leader for boardroom appointments), "essential qualities" of outstanding company chairmen include "charisma, patience, an ability to listen and ability to be supportive".[4] Conversely, characteristics possessed by poor-performing chairmen included the inability to listen, indecisiveness and failure to keep the board on course.

Additionally, good leaders are:

- self-starters;
- good communicators, listeners and networkers who are able to build trust and empathise;

---

[4] The Directorbank Group, "What Makes an Outstanding Chairman? The views of more than 400 directors".

- accessible and approachable;
- confident decision makers and troubleshooters;
- passionate about providing an excellent service that goes beyond the call of duty to their customers and creating an excellent environment for their people to work in;
- knowledgeable about the company's core values, priorities and direction;
- knowledgeable about the industry and the business; and
- insightful about process and politics, reporting and risk.

Additionally, for family businesses, board members must also be able to demonstrate some level of cultural understanding of, and sensitivity to, the family and its business. If they have previously been on boards, they will have had a duty of responsibility to the shareholders of that company. They must also understand, however, that a family business may be different and an openness towards the family's influence on the business is required. They should be able to address and view issues from the perspective of the family and have a firm grasp of the family's policies and approach to governance, as set out in the family charter or constitution.

Identifying the Right Board Members

Once you have identified the type of director the business needs, how do you match that 'ideal candidate' description to a real person? There are a number of sources available:

- **Investors** make great board members as they have a vested interest in looking after the interests of the company.
- **External company boards** – look towards those companies in other industries you admire and invite their CEOs to join your board.
- **Partners and customers** – it makes good business sense to start with the network of people and contacts with whom the company already trades. These candidates can have a good depth of knowledge about the business and have the benefit of having watched it trade and grow from 'outside', thus bringing an objective view of the operation onto the board.
- **Headhunters at executive agencies** – agencies will know the people with the right skill set, level of ambition and industry

expertise and will do all they can to understand your objectives and requirements for growth.

- **Online services** such as DirectorBank.com, TheFDcentre.co.uk or BoardMatch.ie.

Case Study: Fluidata – NED Board Members[5]

Piers Daniell runs Fluidata, an award-winning data delivery network business that delivers innovative high-speed data connectivity solutions to the corporate, industry and public sectors based in the UK. His non-executive director came from his own contact network; a person he respected, trusted and knew had the right expertise to make a good contribution.

"My NED, Larry Viner, was my first customer when I was 15 years old and running my own IT consultancy business fixing computers at weekends. Larry ran a number of businesses in North London and when we had all the issues with the investors, he came in at that stage."

The non-executive chairman (NEC) is also a trusted advisor: "He's my stepfather, Joachim. He's been working in the City for a long time and been involved in a number of companies, from Rio Tinto and some chemical and mining companies. As my family now has a vested interest in the business, it works well that he can do a quarterly review."

This works well for Fluidata because the NED has a small business mentality and understanding and the NEC has a more corporate mindset. "It's a nice contrast," Piers says.

How to Get the Most from the Board

- Define expectations clearly from the outset in terms of frequency and duration of board meetings and whether directors will be expected to prepare for meetings. Outline the kind of dynamic

---

[5] Daniell, P. Interview with Cheryl Rickman (February 2010).

you are seeking in the boardroom and whether you'd prefer directors to play 'devil's advocate' and question your decisions, or merely give advice and act as a sounding board.

- Provide information to educate the members about your business and how it works, from organisation charts, biographies of the management team and financials to marketing collateral and site visits – whatever will help give them a better understanding about the business and how it operates.

- Consider areas where you may give up some control in order to get more from your board and their wealth of expertise, making their responsibilities as meaningful as possible. For example, from seeking their approval on major investments, executive compensation and significant capital expenditure to corporate policies, dividends, benefits and distributions, the more impact they can have, the more they will make a positive difference to the business going forward.

- Prepare well for board meetings and set a clear and meaningful agenda that involves exploratory discussion rather than just presentations. Distribute background materials and the agenda in advance to enable preparation by all attendees. Focus on the future rather than taking up the majority of time reviewing the past.

- Hold an annual board 'away day' to discuss long-term strategic issues and cover a lot of important ground.

- Invite members of the executive management team to present to the board on occasion. Make sure to allow sufficient time after such presentations for the board to discuss it with the executive involved, and for closed discussion thereafter, if necessary.

- Keep lines of communication open between board members and family owners. Shareholders' interests, concerns and expectations must be represented, so create opportunities for formal and informal interaction between owners and board members. From annual dinners and shareholders' meetings to informal lunches and shared board meeting agendas, use every opportunity to give owners an insight into what issues are currently under the spotlight.

- Assess the performance of the board by enabling each member to carry out a self-evaluation and overall evaluation of the performance of the board. When evaluating themselves, board members should assess whether they are able to assess the company's financial performance, understand what the company does well and not so well when compared with its competitors, and understand markets within which the company operates. They should also assess whether or not they have based their actions on shareholders' interests, are willing to disagree with management or the chairman and how often they attend board meetings. When evaluating the board overall, the board should: assess whether or not it assumes a role of oversight or management; how organised and productive board members are; whether it is structured to gain maximum contribution from members; and whether opinions are clearly expressed and issues thoroughly and effectively discussed.

In Part III we have examined the importance of establishing governance structures for your family business. As each business is unique, there is no standard governance model, but it should now be clear that governance is necessary, beneficial and worth the time and resources you will devote to it. The framework of a business is its guiding line, setting out the ways in which business will be done and is expected to be done. To this end, the policies and principles of governance are important tools with which you must equip management and staff. Following this discussion of how to do business effectively and fairly, we will now turn to how to do business into the future and succeed in the long term.

Appendix 7.1: Appointing Authorities to the Board

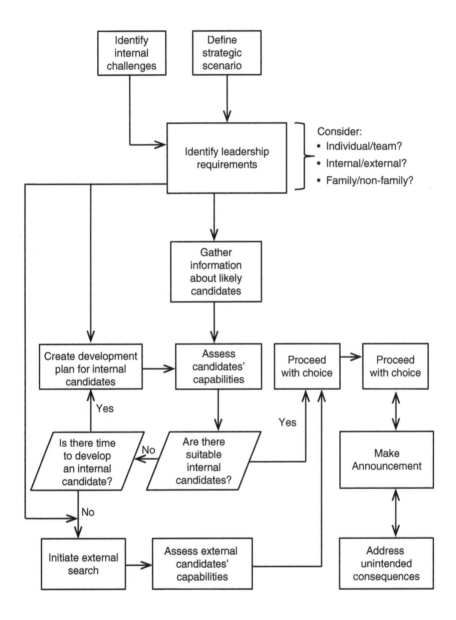

Part IV

The Future of the Business

CHAPTER 8

Engaging the Next Generation

Introduction

Thus far, we have examined the founding motivation and principles of the family business, the drive to succeed of the first-generation owners, the basis of a successful family business and how to professionalise it. This has built up a coherent picture of the advantages of a family business and the ways in which a well-run company can benefit the family that owns it.

Some might still question, however, the need to involve children and grandchildren – should an entrepreneur just focus on establishing and building the business, and then leave his or her progeny to find their own way in life? Would that be easier all round? The truth is that a family business that is well organised, striving for excellence, guided by a strong vision and a passion for the work can be an enormously satisfying place to work. There is also the sense of a collective achievement, of a baton being passed from generation to generation, connecting them over time. These can be powerful incentives to become part of the family business. This chapter will examine the role of the next generation, advising on how best to incorporate the young blood into the family tradition, and benefit from the qualities they bring with them.

Why Bring in the Next Generation?

It is important for senior members and leaders of a family business to consider how valuable the members of the next generation are and what might happen without them. Companies that don't engage the next generation or ignore their talents could lose their best assets for creating a sustainable long-term business. The next generation should be valued for bringing:

- **A wealth of new experiences, enthusiasm and innovations** If they worked for a time in other companies and have gained experience externally, next-generation business members can bring contacts, people-focused skills, plus an injection of fresh enthusiasm and innovation.

- **Renewed confidence in the business** Everyone gains confidence about the long-term future of the business when the next generation is given the chance to shine and bring fresh ideas and energy to a business. It might also signal to staff and contractors that the business will remain in the family rather than being sold.
- **Technological know-how** The next generation tends to be more at home with technology, particularly those who have grown up in the digital world. To them, phones have always been mobile and the Internet has always been there. They can enable instant and improved communication by adopting technologies and approaches with which they are already familiar. For example, they might introduce the efficiencies of a 'paperless office'. Harnessing technological advantages in this way will give the business a competitive advantage.

Getting the Next Generation Involved

It usually requires a delicate balance to encourage the involvement of the next generation in the business, while at the same time not making them feel strangled by the pressure to join. These pressures can differ from person to person. Some might feel it is not the career path for them and resent the weight of expectation the family business places on them. Others might enjoy their involvement but fear failure, being the one to 'mess it all up' after all the hard work done and gains made by their predecessors. This fear is articulated by Melanie Freebody, a second-generation joint-managing director of the Peter Freebody & Co boatyard in Hurley, Berkshire, on the River Thames: "The drive is about keeping it going. If you've grown up with it all your life, the feeling that it might not be there in the future is too terrible to think about."[1]

It is important to note that successors who don't feel pressured to join the family firm may actually develop a stronger sense of ownership of the business than those who do feel under pressure. The question then is: how can the senior members or leaders of a family business

---

[1] Wallop, H., "They're 300 years old and still in business". *The Telegraph*, 1 January 2013.

inspire and engage the next generation to want to join the business without putting them under pressure, thus encouraging them to take genuine *ownership*?

The most common approach is to involve the next generation matter-of-factly and without fuss from an early age. They typically get involved after secondary school or college, with many already having worked in the family business during summer holidays over the years, giving them a good feel for the business. In order to build on this natural progression:

- Create a career development plan for the next generation, including scheduled training and education, such as school/college/holiday experience at the family firm, participation in a new start-up, practical training courses and formal education, or working on family projects (such as a presentation summarising the business vision and indicating examples of that vision through the various stages of development).
- Invite them to join the family council or attend family council meetings on occasion. Ask them for their opinions on certain matters. Show that their input is asked for and valued. Inviting them to participate engages them in a meaningful way, which should have a very positive impact.
- Achieve the right balance between support and independence. If you provide too much support, they are less likely to feel pride in their accomplishments and their level of commitment may be hampered; with not enough support, they may feel lost, disappointed and discouraged.

The key outcome from this approach is to imbue the next generation with the sense that the family firm is an open and welcoming environment in which they are invited to play a meaningful role. In this way, the family firm becomes a positive option that they can 'opt into', rather than a noose around their necks, cutting off other options. It must feel to them like a route they have chosen themselves, and one that they will succeed in only through hard work.

Related to this is the need to educate the current generation about how to interact with the next generation, i.e. how to follow the approach outlined above. For this to work, every family member must respect the decisions of all other individuals and give them the space they need to make those decisions. The current generation often looks at its successors in despair, considering them to be too immature or inexperienced to be entrusted with the family's precious work. If we look at an example we are by now familiar with – M I Dickson Ltd – we see how the next generation can surprise everyone when given the power to be completely involved in running the business. It is a lesson all current-generation owners would be wise to take note of, perhaps using it to examine their own prejudices about their successors.

CASE STUDY: M I DICKSON LTD – EARNING CREDIBILITY DURING DIFFICULT TIMES[2]

Siblings Michael and Christine Dickson were thrust into their leadership roles as teenagers, following the untimely death of their father in 1966. However, while they had no formal preparation, the business was 'in their blood' from a very early age, as Michael describes:

"There really wasn't any particular division between home and work, particularly in the very early days, because when I was an infant my family literally lived above the shop. Mum and dad were there of course, but so was my favourite aunt, mum's sister, and favourite uncle, dad's brother, who worked there; even my father's mother, my lovely granny, helped out.

"Our small additional staff were part of my extended family, and when you remember that sense of love and security in an environment where there was always something good to eat and your senses were assaulted by the smells of baking and roasting, it always felt like a good place to be. Current concepts of a work/life balance viewed through the rose-tinted lenses of my formative years still seem like something of a foreign concept, but the demands of a 24 hours a day, seven days per week food business can often test that idealised view, as it's bloody demanding!"

Michael and Christine struggled to learn the business, and also with the assumptions of staff members who couldn't see how a

---

[2] Dickson, M. Interview with author (July 2013).

couple of teenagers could effectively be their 'bosses'. There came a turning point, however, when Michael was in his early twenties:

"We had a real problem in our bakery and I knew in my heart there was only one way to solve it – we needed to remove a really disruptive influence. Everyone in the business was intimidated by this person, including me! It may sound melodramatic, but I've always seen what happened as a turning point. If I hadn't taken my courage in both hands and removed this person, we could never have moved on and the positive concept of identifying challenges and dealing with them would never have taken root. I firmly believe that. It showed everyone my determination, if initial hesitancy, to run the business and that we youngsters had come of age."

After that, the atmosphere gradually changed and people were pleased that Michael had taken control.

"In the years immediately following my dad's death, we tried everything we could to make a profit, but the business seemed to be unravelling without him. The cry of 'your dad wouldn't have done that' not only served to remind me he wasn't there, but it chipped away at your confidence and self-belief that you could actually turn things around.

"Despite the series of positive changes introduced to try to get the business back on track, Chris and I were used to getting bad news at our visits to our father's old accountant. So we could barely believe it when, with our thin understanding of the accounts, he suggested that we should consider taking a distribution of profits: our efforts were beginning to pay off and we were dumbstruck but delighted!"

Within six years they had their first small factory and within another 10 they had moved into a new, larger-scale factory. Michael's buy-and-build strategy worked:

"We needed to bring additional income streams into the business to cover the significant increase in overheads the new building would bring, so we made a conscious decision to expand the small amount of wholesale work we were doing at the time. I bought two small wholesale businesses and moved their production into the new facility. Now, 20 years on, while our retail estate of 25 shops provides better margins, volume sales in the wholesale division have outstripped those in the traditional business."

Preparing the Next Generation

The family can play a very significant role in preparing the next generation for the challenges and complexities of running the business. They need to be taught the value of money; they will need a strong work ethic and a sense of self-reliance and capability; they will need confidence in their abilities; and they will need to benefit from the experience of those who have gone before by being told about the strengths and weaknesses, successes and failures of the company. In order to do their job right and grow the business, they will need a wide and varied skill set. For example, they must be able to: analyse and understand financial statements, capital structure and corporate strategy; make mission-critical decisions and steer the company forward; and have a firm grounding in how the business generates and spends cash and know its cash flow position in order to maintain accountability among managers, align shareholder and management interests and assess value of the business at any point. It is a daunting task, so preparation is essential to enable the next generation to feel equal to the challenge.

It is wise to instruct the next generation in the following areas:

- How money must be earned, saved and invested. Do this from an early age so that they understand its value.
- How the family made its fortune and the hard work that has gone into accumulating wealth; how decisions are made about how to spend, save or invest that wealth.
- What might happen if poor decisions were made about how to spend, save or invest and why taking responsibility is so important.

- Allocate a budget for training and then work out a learning plan with the next generation to include training materials, peer groups, conferences, evening classes, webinars, etc.
- Achieve the right balance between *opportunities* and *responsibilities*, to prepare the next generation to inherit and manage wealth well and avoid an attitude of entitlement. Do this by instilling values about working hard and persevering, showcasing achievements and celebrating the family's past, but also by explaining that money brings responsibilities. Importantly, the younger generation must understand that wealth does not necessarily bring credibility, which must also be earned.
- Teach them the importance of seeking consensus, for example by participating in the family council. Invite them to join the occasional family council meeting, take notes and look for the consensus.
- Finally, consider financing their entrepreneurial spirit if they choose to start their own business.

Understanding the Stages of Personal and Professional Development

The founders of family businesses have fires in their bellies, the entrepreneurial spirit and a dogged determination to succeed. The next generation will need to develop this same passion and persistence in order to continue to drive the business, make it work and grow it significantly. It is good practice for them to try to gain work experience outside the family business, within the area they most enjoy, are good at and have the most passion for, and bring this experience back to the family business if and when they join.

Generally, as children grow from teenagers into young adults and parents are in their forties or fifties, parents tend to be more willing and able to act as mentors, offering plenty of support and encouragement. The younger generation, for their part, are more open to being mentored. However, as people grow older and life cycles and stages of development shift, the generation gap widens. One decade later, as the 'children' enter their thirties and the parents are in their mid to late fifties or sixties, the younger generation may have become entirely independent and successful in their own right; they may feel that they no longer need to be mentored and will strive to have more control. At this juncture, neither parent may be ready to relinquish much control of the business, feeling that the potential successor is not yet competent enough to take over. These conflicting stages of development can be further complicated by external life factors, for example where the son or daughter wants to buy a larger house for his or her growing family and needs a bigger salary from the family business, while the parents' financial focus is adding to their retirement pot.

Indeed, the stages of individual development can cause havoc for family businesses, primarily because two individuals, especially from different generations, are at different stages of growth and therefore have very different needs. For example, after leaving college the next generation may have a vision of their future and start to work. As they progress into the adult world they will start to explore possibilities and seize opportunities. Their focus may then shift from work to focusing on relationships and then settling down and becoming successful in their own right. The next stage will be the transition to midlife, where they start to commit to new or reaffirm existing choices in their life and begin to create a legacy. As retirement approaches, the next phase often involves a struggle to remain youthful while the body starts to say otherwise, as well as the need to pass authority on to the younger generation.

Meanwhile, the business will be moving through a developmental stage of its own: from an era of central control by one person at the top, to one of delegation, where managers are employed to take on tasks while still allowing the founder to maintain an element of control. Delegation enables the entrepreneur to work *on* the business rather than *in* it; to focus on strategic growth and sustainability. Navigating through these developmental stages of the business can prove difficult for the entrepreneur at the helm when it is coupled with their own life development.

There can be various points of conflict between the business, family and individual life stages, illustrated by a few examples below:

- Frustration on the part of a son or daughter, who feel they are being held back from taking on more responsibility, demonstrating their competence and establishing credibility. On the other side, the parent may feel that the son or daughter is being unappreciative and disrespectful by expecting or demanding more from the business. The relationship between the parent and child deteriorates and there is a risk that the most likely (and most closely involved) successor will leave.

- The business is at a stage that requires delegation as well as new systems to support development, without which growth could stall and value could be limited. Sooner or later an entrepreneur must realise that he or she cannot do everything and should put in place a management team, which must then be left to get on with the job.

- The owner of the family business will have significantly more experience than their adult children. Psychologically, the owner will always see their adult children as *children*. Meanwhile, children, even as adults, do not want to disappoint their parents. They want to meet their parents' expectations, but they also need to satisfy their own dreams and do what they love. The balance needs to be right for the next generation to thrive.

The potential for conflict and dissatisfaction means that these life stages must be considered and planned for in advance so that they can be managed effectively and for the good of the business. Advice on how to prevent and manage the kinds of conflict that can arise between the different generations in a family business is set out below.

HOW TO PREVENT AND/OR MANAGE CONFLICT ARISING FROM DIFFERING LIFE STAGES

- **Reach a compromise** For example, establish a new division of the business and hand over enough responsibility to the next generation that they will be able to make a contribution, thus retaining their passion and not being frustrated in their efforts to forge a credible career.

- **Talk** Throughout this book we've focused on the need for open and honest communication. Discuss goals, concerns, hopes and fears and tackle them patiently, with empathy for one another's point of view.

- **Avoid favouritism** Family members cannot be seen as being treated more favourably than other staff, as this would be hugely divisive and could result in loss of staff. Patrick Buckley, Deputy MD of EPS Group, emphasises the importance of this: "We worked in the business and weren't preferred in terms of positions or titles or jobs. You came in at the bottom and worked your way up and worked in different parts of the business and were treated the same as any employee…Then you'd move into different positions depending on an opportunity as it arose, and that'll be no different for the third generation."[3]

- **Empower the next generation with freedom to define their own path** Give them choice rather than obligation.

- **Enable the next generation to cultivate their interests and passions** If they could do anything in life, what would they choose to do? What unique contribution would they like to make to the world?

- **Encourage them to assess their current skills, strengths and weaknesses** What gaps would they like to fill in their skills, experience and knowledge? What are they hungry to learn about? What achievements are they most proud of? Self-awareness bolsters self-belief. Give them feedback on their abilities and help them figure out what they should do next in order to develop and grow in the right direction.

- **Empower them** Encourage them to gain skills and credibility through training and career development opportunities before they join the firm (*if* they join the firm).

- **Enable them to build confidence and gain skills and contacts in the outside world** Ideally, they should work outside of the family business before joining it full-time. This builds self-confidence and helps to overcome any feelings of entitlement or obligation. They should only fill a vacancy that actually exists.

- **Make the next generation aware that you have a 'Plan B'** should they choose not to join the firm, i.e. you will seek to bring in outside professionals instead. It is important that there is no 'guilt' attached to Plan B.

---

[3] Buckley, P. Interview with author (July 2013).

- **Think outside the box and embrace change** Allow the next generation to make their own mark on the business.

- **Communicate openly and often about risk versus opportunity** We already know the vital importance of open and frequent communication. Chatting informally about marketing ideas, strategy, risk and overcoming obstacles is a worthwhile pursuit in engaging the next generation. Often, where the senior generation sees risk, the younger generation will see opportunity. Discuss how these might be balanced and compromises reached.

- **Devote time to building the next generation's confidence and level of skills, experience and knowledge** Do this by giving them the chance to take on responsibilities that will enable them to experience both success and failure first hand, develop projects from idea to execution, work on governance processes, manage risk and perform due diligence. Have them work alongside a professional advisor or mentor, but allow them to take the lead.

- **Give them more responsibility over time** Increase their level of responsibility; give them the opportunity to run their own department or division of the business and get involved in strategic planning. Assign them to various jobs on a rotation basis to learn the ropes across a variety of roles (and consider where there might be room for improvement once they do take the helm).

- **Give them the chance to develop** Help them improve their decision-making skills, leadership abilities, interpersonal skills and risk orientation. The only way to gain proficiency in these areas is to make decisions, lead and take risks.

- **Encourage them to assess the viability of their ideas within the marketplace** Consider the resources they would need to make their ideas work, figure out who might be best placed to lead or help take an idea through to fruition.

- **Encourage them explore growth areas for the business** What product ranges might they expand or markets might they expand into? How might they invest in innovation or grow the geographical footprint of the business?

What if the Next Generation *Does* Wish to Join the Family Business?

When a next-generation relative takes the decision to join the family business, this is a time for careful planning. There are pitfalls to be avoided, just as there are opportunities to be grasped. It is important that the transition is handled sensitively and sensibly for the good of all concerned – shareholders, the owner, the next generation and existing staff members, both family and non-family. The following guidelines should help make the process as smooth as possible:

- Offer the next generation short-term learning opportunities early, e.g. through part-time work and work experience, for one or two weeks at a time to give them a chance to learn the basics of the business.
- Clearly define expectations, hours, performance requirements and responsibilities, as well as project objectives and reporting lines.
- Ensure that non-family managers will nurture their strengths and praise their accomplishments while also providing critical feedback on areas that could be improved.
- Allow room for growth. Don't start your son or daughter in a position that is beyond their knowledge and skillset. This could lead to their credibility taking a bashing, along with their self-confidence. Let them work their way up like anyone else would.
- Match skills and interests and passion with the role.
- Enable them to gain experience in all departments, if possible. Provide a mixture of operational and staff experience. Ensure they gain exposure to various aspects of the company.
- Give them 360-degree feedback reports from everyone, including peers as well as managers or direct reports. Then create a development plan that encourages strengths and addresses weaknesses.
- Involve non-family managers and external advisors in decisions around promoting next-generation family members.
- Give the next generation every opportunity to build-confidence and self-esteem, demonstrate their competencies and learn on the job.
- Avoid favouritism, but also avoid riding roughshod over them to show other employees that you are not exhibiting favouritism. Try to find the midpoint between these two extremes.

CHAPTER 9

Women in Family Businesses

The history of women in family businesses is an interesting one. Until the late 1900s, the story was depressingly unchanging: women provided crucial support to the family business, devoted their time and energy to it, reared the next generation, but were overlooked when it came to ownership or leadership and were undervalued from home to office. The family business – as all other types of business – was the male domain and women were expected to work hard but remain on the margins. The unquestioned system of primogeniture saw sons groomed and pushed forward for inclusion, promotion and success, while a daughter's worth was measured in marriage prospects. This remained the status quo for a long time, but from the 1970s – when Ireland joined the EEC (now EU) – it became apparent that things were changing. Yes, it came slowly, but it came nonetheless and in the past fifteen years the speed of that change has accelerated, bringing with it a vital new role for women in the family business.

In the 1960s and 1970s women worked mainly in the home undertaking the household and childcare duties. The civil service even operated the 'marriage bar', whereby once a woman got married, she had to give up her job and become a full-time homemaker. The underlying assumption was that this was what women wanted, and government and society were simply helping them to fulfil those ambitions. This assumption has affected women's lives for a long time, both professionally and socially. It would seem that women were assigned the role of notional 'head of the family', but were not seen to have any entitlement to be 'head of the business'.

The historical assumption that the male family members would inherit the business and the women would support them was hugely damaging to the family business, as it denied so many businesses the benefit of men and women working together to create a sustainable enterprise. We now know that women make a huge contribution at the boardroom table; it's just unfortunate it has taken so long for this new chapter in the story to be written. However, there is only limited scope in looking back and lamenting; the important thing is to look at the present and plan for a better future.

What has Changed?

The last 20 years have seen major developments in the story of women in the family business. The next generation of women professionals, now toiling away in secondary school, will likely have a very different view of their futures and potential than their grandmothers had. The key change has been education, particularly women's increased access to third-level education. Current statistics show that women are now more likely to hold a third-level qualification than men, which is a major U-turn in a relatively short period of time. This means that men can no longer claim special knowledge or ability in business. Education has levelled the playing field and women have been quick to take advantage. Women family members are now very likely to hold a degree and to have gained experience working with other employers prior to entering the family business. This gives them an important asset in terms of gaining skill sets and broad experience, making them more valuable to the family business and more confident about their ability to make a significant contribution to it. Education gives a person confidence, which has been a stumbling block for women in the workplace. As a result, more and more daughters are stepping forward and demanding to be considered for senior and managerial roles in family businesses.

It takes time to change mindsets, but women have been forging new paths and careers right across the board. Ireland has had women presidents and has a woman attorney general – there are now role models in the highest positions in the land. This is crucial for rewriting the old story and proving that women are capable professionals and that much is to be gained from men and women working side by side. In terms of the family business, this means that succession is no longer male dominated – the focus is now on the choosing right successor, regardless of gender.

What Needs to Change?

In order for women to have equal opportunities and a chance to find out what they can do in the business, there are issues that still need to be addressed and changes that still need to be made. One of the key areas that must be addressed is salary. In research conducted in 2000, Rowe and Hong found that while women's contribution to the family business was substantial and important and necessary, they were nonetheless paid the lowest salaries.[1] This is still reflected across business in general, with women today earning on average 14.4% less than their male counterparts. While there are women at the top of their professions who are very wealthy, there is work to be done in tackling the chauvinism that allows workers to be paid less solely because of their gender. The family business can lead the charge in this regard, ensuring that all staff members – family and non-family – are assessed objectively and fairly and paid according to their position and merits. It makes good business sense to work within an equal framework.

Another key issue that affects many women is the issue of combining family life and career. There comes a point when the question of children or no children has to be answered. For career women, this can be a complicated question, with the unpleasant feeling of having to make a 'choice'. This is a very broad issue, involving many interconnected elements, but it is becoming more and more critical that government policy moves with the times and provides legislation that will more effectively protect women's careers and promote women in business, taking into account women's need for flexibility regarding family obligations. There has been work done in this area to date, but more discussion and action is required.

There will always be obstacles to overcome, but it is important to examine them in terms of solutions rather than the problems they create. So the key questions to ask are: 'What can women do to effect the necessary changes?' and 'What can the family business do to effect the necessary changes?'

---

[1] Rowe, B.R. and Hong, G.S., "The role of wives in family business: The paid and unpaid work of women" (2000) Vol. 13 No. 1 *Family Business Review*.

What Can Women Do to Effect Change?

In her 2013 book, *Lean In*, Sheryl Sandberg, COO of Facebook, argued that women must start from a position that work and family life can be combined and then 'lean in' to give themselves – and to take – every opportunity for advancement in the workplace. She was referring to women in all types of business, and it is equally good advice for daughters when choosing where they might fit in to the family enterprise.

It is striking that in Ireland, nearly twice as many men as women start businesses. This suggests that women either lack confidence, or lack access to capital, or are put off by the seemingly impossible demands of having a solid home life alongside a successful work life. Sandberg argues that women should identify their own personal and professional ambitions and do everything possible to achieve them. It is necessary that women refuse to accept any mindset or policy that seeks to side-line them because they are mothers too.

There are, of course, many trailblazers and role models in Ireland who have already cleared a path for women in business, such as Darina Allen of Ballymaloe and Marian O'Gorman of the Kilkenny Group, and their insights and advice are valuable. In a 2014 report, Coutts & Co highlighted the changing role of women in the family business – showing that the family business is now 48% more likely to have women on its board of directors than non-family business. It also listed 10 key points for women to be aware of, courtesy of women who have gone before:

"1. Don't try to change too much, too quickly when you first join – even if you see some obvious recommendations that need to be made.
2. Gaining experience outside the family business can help ensure you are taken seriously and will give you something to bring back to the business.
3. Discuss and align your vision with family members to ensure you're driving the business together in the same direction.
4. Ensure family values are reflected in the way the business is run.
5. Network with other family business owners to understand their governance and how they do things.

6. Be conscious of others around you who may be confused by the closeness between family members and how you make decisions and manage your differences naturally.
7. Agree how decisions will be made and how differences of opinion will be managed with other family members.
8. Set boundaries between work and home and agree clear roles and responsibilities in both.
9. Utilise non-family management and external advisers to help mentor and bridge the gap between different generations.
10. Think outside the box and embrace change. When the time comes, allow the next generation to make their own mark on the business."[2]

What Can the Family Business Do to Effect Change?

Where once the family business was guilty of keeping women in the shadows, it is now operating in the vanguard of a change sweeping the business world. It used to be the case that women, when included at all, were pushed into 'people skills' roles, such as HR. That is now changing, and women are increasingly making their presence felt in the boardroom – as executive and non-executive directors and as owners. There is also a growing network of support structures for women. For example, Julie Sinnamon, the current CEO of Enterprise Ireland, and her colleagues are actively focusing on women's entrepreneurship and employment. Furthermore, research has shown that a diversified board, comprising male and female members, is the most successful model, producing greater focus on problem solving and effective decision making.

In terms of family business owners, there is much that can be done to ensure that all family members have equal opportunities. It is important to treat the business as a whole-family concern, encouraging all of the next generation to see it as a potential career. The more potential candidates for succession, the better for the business – provided the best candidate is chosen based on experience, skills and proven ability. It can be the case that the

[2] Coutts & Co, *Dedication – Portraits of Women in Family Business*, 2010.

father–daughter relationship is easier to work within. One woman CEO made this point in a research study, arguing that there is less ego involved than in the father–son relationship, which can make succession easier to plan and manage. This will not apply to every family business, of course, but it is an interesting angle on the psychology of succession.

It is important for the owner to be a strong leader and to promote equality throughout the business, from the top down. The concept of equality should form part of the company's mission and values statement, so that all staff members feel equally valued and know that promotions and advancement will be based solely on performance and results. Successful women in business have the power to influence thinking and normalise women's advancement to positions of leadership and ownership.

The family business would seem a natural place for a woman to excel in her career. She will have the determination and focus borne of the family conviction and will to succeed, plus the insider knowledge of family dynamics and personalities. Contrary to the outdated traditional opinion, women can be superior leaders – instinctive, lateral thinkers and quick to admit when they are wrong and something new needs to be tried. These qualities are evident, for example, in the case studies about Darina Allen and Marian O'Gorman below. It should also be the case that, as the family and business are so closely intertwined, the question of childcare and flexibility should be easier to resolve for all concerned.

The Future of Women in Family Business

It is to be welcomed that the family business sector is spearheading the move towards greater equality. This is particularly important given that the sector is so strong in terms of economic performance, employment and marketing. These changes to mindset, outlook and company make-up will filter across business and through to society, making the family business an important engine for change. This movement is widespread – for example, a US family business survey in 1997 found that 4.7% had women CEOs and that 19.2% of family employees were women; when the same questions were posed ten years later in 2007, 24% had women CEOs and 40% of family employees were women. These are very healthy figures and they are continuing to go in the right direction.

It is very good for business that the value of women family members is finally being recognised. All the research points to the benefits of having women involved at all levels of business and highlights the contributions women can bring to the table. Now that women have such strong role models to follow, it should be the case that women can truly take their place at the boardroom table and help to create thriving family businesses.

In May 2014, the *Irish Independent* published an impressive list of businesswomen entitled, "The 50 most influential and powerful women in business". Such a list would have been unimaginable even 30 years ago, and it stands as a testament to the tenacity, ability and ambition of women in business. Among those fifty were included Margaret Heffernan and Sharon McMahon of Dunnes Stores, Caroline Keeling of Keelings Fruit and Marion O'Gorman of the Kilkenny Group – hopefully many more family businesswomen will join their ranks soon.

CASE STUDY: DARINA ALLEN AND THE BALLYMALOE FAMILY BUSINESS[3]

Darina Allen established the Ballymaloe Cookery School in 1983 with her brother, Rory O'Connell. She has written 18 cookery books and presented nine series of her TV programme, *Simply Delicious*. She has worked hard to establish the Ballymaloe Cookery School, which is now internationally recognised as one of the top academies in the world for aspiring chefs. Her family business employs 72 people and doesn't have a PR company – it's all word of mouth. When your business is this good, it speaks for itself.

Darina Allen is, she confesses, completely at home in the family business set-up. She was born into a family business and then married into one, becoming Myrtle Allen's daughter-in-law and second in line to the oven at Ballymaloe House. For Darina, there

---

[3] Based on an interview with the author, July 2014.

are huge benefits to running a family business. She enjoys the deeper level of commitment she and the other family members feel towards the business, the sense of pride in their achievements, the stronger element of humanity in what they do and how they do it, the personal touch and the sense that they are giving back to their community – both locally and nationally.

One of the cornerstones of the Ballymaloe family business is its clear and vital business vision and philosophy. The motto they work by is to promise less and give more to their customers. Accordingly, Darina urges other family businesses to "charge enough for your product and be realistic about the real cost of delivering a quality product rather than compromising on selling price and then not delivering to customers, which leaves people in a permanent state of disappointment." It's very good advice, and it's clear to see that it has stood the Allen family in good stead down through the years.

Allied to this core vision is the Quaker ethos that quietly informs the workings of the family business. 'Honesty, integrity, simplicity, equality and peace are central to the way we conduct our lives,' Darina notes, going on to point out that Quaker women were always educated and it was taken for granted that women were equal to men in every way. That sense of fairness, equal opportunity and plain decency in all dealings is apparent in every facet of Ballymaloe, and it is responsible for the loyalty exhibited by the family's customers, students, staff and suppliers.

When asked about their recipe for success, Darina cites communication as a vital component of the family business. They have specific structures in place to ensure the business is run professionally and efficiently. Once a week, Darina, her brother Rory, husband Tim, and son Toby conduct a meeting to examine issues and monitor progress. Minutes are kept of these meetings and actions noted and delegated to the appropriate staff. There is also a quarterly meeting involving the immediate family, at which all manner of issues can be raised and discussed in a forum that is open, inclusive and friendly. Darina also notes that the family members have lots of informal discussions throughout the day – always keeping one another updated on developments. This ongoing communication is essential to keeping everyone involved and ensure any potentially contentious issues are dealt with quickly and effectively. She concedes that at present they do not have a family constitution underpinning the business, but they have worked out structures for the day-to-day running of the business. Through good communication, all parties have a solid understanding and working knowledge of the business and how it is conducted. There is, Darina says, a huge bond of trust in their family business.

This all sounds wonderfully amicable and smoothly efficient, but the business does, of course, face difficult issues from time to time. When asked about how they deal with conflict, Darina has clear ideas and advice. Talking is the key method – ongoing positive communication that involves all parties. Darina says it is essential that people don't bottle things up and allow them to grow into even bigger problems. Accordingly, at Ballymaloe they have an 'open table' policy in more ways than one – urging family members and staff to bring all issues to the meeting table quickly, safe in the knowledge that it is an open space where they will be heard. Darina and Rory will often ask family members to reflect on these discussions and return the following day with their thoughts – an important break that allows people to consider matters in detail and allows emotions to settle, so that logic and good business sense can prevail. At Ballymaloe, it is essential, Darina says, to make enough time to communicate properly (which is always a challenge).

As an example of how they deal with potentially difficult issues, Darina cites the decision to invite her son, Toby, to join the business. An IT specialist, Toby joined the business in 2012 as a prospective MD, having relocated from Scotland. Darina has always held that the subject of a family member joining the business must be discussed in depth and at length, especially if he or she is married. This adds a tricky complication that must be confronted head-on and discussed openly, which is how they approached the proposal to bring Toby on board. It wasn't taken as a given simply because he was Darina's son; he had to present his case and it was discussed in detail before a decision was taken. As Darina says, there is too much at stake to do otherwise. It is essential to establish that the family member in question has the right temperament to join the team and he or she must also show commitment to going out and gaining any skills they need to bring to their role. In Toby's case, the discussion had a favourable outcome and he is now enjoying the challenge of steering the business into the future.

Another essential ingredient for Darina is openness to change – a quality so often missing from family businesses. At Ballymaloe, they are conscious of not allowing complacency to creep into their thinking. For example, at present they don't have any non-executive directors, but they haven't ruled out appointing these roles in the future if the need arises. Also, while Darina's daughters are not currently involved in the business, there is an awareness that they may wish to join in the future, and this change will be welcomed and discussed just like any other. Crucially, Darina is very open to changing how they do business and what they offer to customers, which led to the opening of the highly successful cookery school and the Ballymaloe Literary Festival of Food and Wine, which has become a highlight on the Irish festivals calendar, attracting big-name chefs and audiences from around the world. It's a perfect example of diversifying into success.

The Ballymaloe business is now looking at welcoming the fourth-generation Allens into the company. Their approach to succession is very positive. Darina says they welcome and encourage new ideas and allow younger members to try out new things, to find out what works. There is a rule underlying that 'have a go' attitude, though: every business under the Ballymaloe umbrella must be financially independent. This ensures that all the eggs are not in one basket, which in turn safeguards all of the ventures operating within the family's remit.

Darina is very aware that succession is an obstacle that has tripped up many a family business. She feels a strong sense of responsibility not only to pass the business on, but to pass it on in good shape and not leave any financial time bombs ticking for the next generation. For its part, the next generation knows what is expected of it and they are involved in ongoing discussions about how the coming years will be planned and how those plans will be implemented. Darina and Rory had the foresight to bring in external advisors to help in this process, which they hope will ensure that it is a successful and efficient transition.

Finally, I asked Darina for advice for others involved in building up family businesses, and she had much to offer. First, don't be afraid of trial and error – this is how she learned to be good at being a family business owner. She admitted that none of her family has formal business training, but they have acquired their considerable skills on the ground, by being hardworking and also humble enough to learn from their mistakes. Secondly, she recommends strongly that you always keep the lines of communication open – avoid silence. It is up to the owners to ensure that anyone with an issue feels confident enough to come forward, secure in the knowledge that they will be heard. Force yourself to take breaks – when people get overtired, problems quickly ensue.

Thirdly, there must be transparency in all business dealings. A good family business has good values, good vision and good ethics. These qualities can only be instilled from the top down, so it is up to the family to ensure that they adhere to the business's codes at all times. Fourth, when a problem arises, find a solution based on working together; and fifth, insist that every business within the family business be financially independent.

Lastly, give one another emotional support. This isn't advice you often see in business books, but as Darina rightly points out, we are dealing with family businesses here, and they should always play to their strengths and acknowledge their foundations. You can be professional while ensuring that every family member working in the business feels part of the bigger dream and goal – that is how you promote succession and keep a business in business over the long term.

CASE STUDY: MARIAN O'GORMAN AND THE KILKENNY GROUP[4]

Marian O'Gorman is CEO of Kilkenny Group, which currently has 13 stores nationwide, 11 Kilkenny stores, two Christy's Irish Stores, two restaurants and a growing online store. The company employs 230 people. Kilkenny originated as a government initiative to support the Irish crafts and design industry. In 1975, her father Christy Kelleher purchased Blarney Woollen Mills. Christy's ethos of looking after customers and staff rubbed off on his daughter, Marian, which helped to grow the business throughout future years. Marian departed from the Blarney Woollen Mills business in 2000. Due to family differences and as part of the settlement, Kilkenny was assigned to her. The driving vision and ethos of Kilkenny in the past 14 years is clear in everything it does: high-quality, Irish-designed products, support for craftspeople, attention to detail and a determined focus on customer needs. These qualities are pushed by Marian through every level of the business, which has helped make Kilkenny one of the most successful family businesses in Ireland with a turnover of €25.5 million in 2014.

Marian O'Gorman is a family business professional – she has been working in family business since the age of 16 and has spearheaded and overseen the strategic moves that have brought such success to the Kilkenny Group. This is perhaps the key to her role as CEO – she leads on strategy and planning, but is also deeply involved in the day-to-day running of the stores and restaurants that fall under the Kilkenny umbrella. She is knowledgeable about every aspect of her business, with experience and insights gained from working behind the counter all the way to the boardroom. She lives and breathes Kilkenny, and it shows. Her decision making is well-informed and efficient, with a constant emphasis on the future and innovation. These are the hallmarks of a successful business owner, and demonstrate the benefits of coming in at the bottom and working up to the top.

---

[4] Based on an interview with the author, July 2014.

Marian is very clear on the best route into the family business for family members. She strongly recommends that those wishing to join the business work elsewhere first, gaining experience, learning new ideas and processes and then bringing that knowledge back with them to the family business. She also stresses the importance of the bottom-to-top model, encouraging family members to start on the shop floor and earn their stripes as they rise through the ranks. This was the path she laid out for her own children, and as a result they are now taking on their family business with as much passion and determination as Marian herself has always shown. She works with her two daughters, Michelle and Melissa, both senior area managers; and with her son, Greg, who heads up Kilkenny's marketing and PR. It is a formula that has served Kilkenny well, producing capable professionals from the family circle.

It might be tempting to view financial success as the major incentive for family business owners, but for Marian it is much more interesting and complex than just money. For her, there is the pride in taking on the family vision and pushing it to its fullest potential, achieving things the previous generation could have only dreamed of. She inherited from her father a strong business reputation and an eye for quality, but she has gone on to make Kilkenny her own, instilling her vision in the company and working hard to expand the business, to innovate and create new opportunities for the group. This is what makes the job so stimulating and worthwhile. Marian admits that she loves the work – every aspect of it – from the shop floor to the boardroom. She was born to sell and truly enjoys engaging with customers and figuring out what they want – usually before they know it themselves. This is another key aspect of a successful family business – you have to 'get' the family vision and ethos but also keep expanding it, and you have to love what you do.

So what are the benefits, if any, of running a family business? Top of Marian's list is her own personal driving force: determination. When you take on a family business, you are carrying the baton until it's time to pass it on, which lends a very real sense of motivation and urgency to the enterprise. No one wants to be the one to drop the baton, which is how Marian describes her own energetic drive to expand the business and seek out new opportunities. She has built a strong business and her ambition is to pass on an even stronger one – that is the first principle of being a good family business owner and it was instilled in her from the very start. While CEOs are always devoted to their work, those working for others simply don't have the same make-up and drive as those who are taking on a family enterprise and improving it.

Another important benefit is that the reputation of the family and business are interlinked, something that has worked in Marian's favour thanks to her father's work in establishing Blarney as a name meaning quality, customer care and value for money. These traits have been passed intact to Kilkenny and are carefully guarded.

The sense of needing and wanting to make a distinct and significant contribution to the business means that family members work extremely hard to create a successful enterprise. Everyone benefits from this ethos – customers, staff and shareholders. This is something Marian can identify in her own children, who have learned from her the value of hard work, strong business ethics and knowing the business inside out. Like her, they are committed to the business in a way that's hard to quantify, but that is essential for the ongoing success of Kilkenny. As Marian says, they expect more from each other as family members working in the business – they demand a very high level of commitment, passion and drive to succeed from all who choose to become involved.

In business, as in life, things do not always run smoothly. The true test of the family business is how it tackles challenges and difficulties. This can range from internal disagreements to external threats, such as recession. In its 51 years, Kilkenny has faced down a host of challenges while preserving family relationships. Marian has very helpful advice on how to manage family and business to the benefit of both. She recommends that, during the working day, the focus is on the business, not on personalities.

Once everyone conducts themselves in a professional manner, any disagreement or difficulty can be overcome. To this end, each family member must know his or her role and fulfil it correctly.

Linked to this is Marian's advice that steps be taken to prevent, or eradicate, any sort of 'blame culture'. Everyone must appreciate that there are different personalities involved, but that each one brings value and contributes to the business. It is to be encouraged that differences or complaints are aired openly, but equally it is essential that all such issues are brought to a positive conclusion through concerted effort.

Kilkenny operates under a board of directors, which meets monthly, supplemented by a quarterly family meeting. While Marian's husband Michael is not involved in the business, he does sit in on the family meetings, which can lend an objective 'outside' view to proceedings when needed. This forum allows family members to raise issues and discuss them together, giving equal weighting to each member's concerns. There are two official performance reviews annually, where work is assessed, appraised and critiqued. Marian promotes a transparent culture of equality and fairness – a factor that is essential, in Marian's view, because Kilkenny is based on an ethos of treating staff fairly, recognising and rewarding good work and promoting loyalty to the company among all staff members. Marian recognises that a major factor contributing to the success of the business is the commitment, loyalty and hard work of all its staff and senior management team. The group is also looking to appoint two non-executive directors to the board, which will further broaden the skill set of the board and lend even more objectivity to decision making.

Perhaps the single most important piece of advice Marian would like to pass on to other family businesses is this: listen, take advice, and bring in expert opinion. She warns against the notion that things should be 'kept in the family', disagreeing with this exclusive approach to business. In her view, the success of Kilkenny owes a huge amount to their ability to ask for advice and take it. For example, she cites her financial director, Mark Sexton, as an important part of the business for his role as a 'sounding board'. She also recommends that all family businesses should seek out strategic advisors who will bring new ideas and angles to discussions and decision making. Marian may be very experienced in her field, but she nonetheless points out that it is essential to be aware of one's own skill set, and get in the expert help necessary to the business. This also means being able to accept when something hasn't worked, and moving on. This is an important asset for any business owner – you can never fall into the trap of thinking, 'I know best'.

As head of a 51-year-old success story, Marian's insights into business and running a family business are based on hard work and common sense. She has shown the vision it takes to bring a family business from the local to the national and international stage – no mean feat in today's saturated retail sector. She recounts that the best piece of advice she ever received was to 'run the company as if you're going to sell it'. That outlook led her to cut costs, focus on the customer and increase profitability – all of the elements on which Kilkenny's success is based. When asked what was the worst advice ever received, she smiles. "Someone told me to shut down the company, that I wouldn't make any money. Imagine if I'd listened to that nonsense!" Imagine, indeed.

As we have seen in **Chapters 8** and **9**, a family business is only as strong as the family that leads it, which is why it is imperative to pass on good business sense and vision to the next generation in order to secure the future of the business. Once you have a committed next generation in place, half the battle is fought and won. The next half can be all-out bloody warfare, however, if the right procedures are not put in place to govern the succession process. The ability of the current owner to encourage and facilitate succession is essential, but all too often the weight of ego and interfamily relationships can crush the enthusiasm out of the process. Accordingly, the next chapter examines how to help the current owner to let go of the reins and promote a smooth and efficient succession plan.

CHAPTER 10

Successful Succession: Reducing Owner Dependency and Relinquishing Control

Introduction

A family business that has been founded and intended as a legacy business – to be passed on down the generations – will eventually face the inevitable fact of succession. At some point, the current generation must give way to the next, and allow them the chance to take the helm. The success and sustainability of the business depends on how this process is planned, handled and executed. If it is managed clumsily or reluctantly, it can pose a huge threat to the business; there is a great deal at stake.

Succession and exit take time, from initial planning to full implementation. If planning is left until the last minute, the business could end up passing into incapable, ill-prepared, unqualified or reluctant hands. Furthermore, potential conflicts that could emerge without adequate planning (in which needs are sufficiently balanced) could result in severe disruption to the business. Uncertainty and a lack of leadership would then impact morale and could affect sales and growth as a result. Essentially, lack of planning for the critical success factor of new leadership, whether that's through succession or sale, could result in the failure and closure of the business.

Succession is a process, and both the family and business will benefit from its careful planning and execution.

There are three essential steps to successful succession planning and execution, which reflect the ordering of this chapter:

1. **Planning** Sitting down to plan succession with the various generations involved, and ensuring that the selection of successors is well-considered and that all factors are rigorously anticipated. Both the current and the next generations should see the succession in a positive light and openly discuss their concerns and aspirations about either leaving or taking on the responsibility of leadership.

2. **Preparation** When a successor has been chosen, it should be decided when the handover is going to happen, and how each department and every member of staff needs to prepare for this.
3. **Transition Management** In order to make the transition process as seamless as possible, it is preferable that the handover occurs before the current owner/manager steps down.

1. Planning

The best-practice approach for succession planning is very clear:

1. Always have a formal succession plan or exit strategy far ahead of time.
2. Seek external, professional advice to help draft this plan.

Yet not all owners of growing businesses have the end in mind when they start out. Some resolutely refuse to countenance the idea of a time when they won't be in charge. As a result, many do not plan their exit or succession until it's too late. Therein lies the key word: **plan**. Succession warrants very careful and considerable planning, and this should form an important part of the overall development strategy for the business.

It is essential to plan ahead for all major changes in the business, yet despite more than 75% of Irish firms (65% of UK firms) being family-owned, less than half have succession plans in place. This is an indictment of owners and their attitudes to the next generation. It is short-sighted in the extreme to fail to plan for succession. The benefits of such planning speak for themselves.

The Benefits of Planning Ahead

Succession planning enables companies to:

- reduce owner dependency, which removes risks and ensures the future prosperity and potential of the firm;
- adequately prepare the best person(s) to take over control and leadership by allowing time to identify and develop potential successors;

- optimise independent value in case a decision is taken to sell the business;
- ensure that the transition runs smoothly – in business, continuity is key and a family business is at its most vulnerable during a period of succession;
- provide financial security for the senior generation so that they are adequately provided for when they retire. Similarly, the younger generation will need assurance that they can earn a good living from the business and not be straddled by loans to buy the shares from family members. It must be a win–win situation for both generations;
- retain key talent (including the most promising potential successors). Indeed, if succession is not considered, talented potential leaders may get tired of waiting to rise to the challenge. Losing your best talent (especially if they are family) must be avoided;
- safeguard and bolster the long-term health and success of the business by revitalising strategy;
- motivate and reward loyal long-term employees who are key to the business, involved in the planning process and who you wish to remain focused and part of the firm as the succession plan is rolled out;
- produce a multigenerational partnership and plan – working closely with the next generation to plan and organise succession is the ideal way to prepare. This way, both sides have input into planning the succession strategy, which means the current generation will feel reassured and the next generation will feel challenged and excited; and
- reap the rewards through wealth preservation and seizing the opportunities that being part of a family business creates.

Succession planning should not be narrow-minded. It is important to consider scenarios other than the obvious ones, i.e. the sale of the business or the retirement of the owner. When setting out to plan for such eventualities, it is necessary to also pose a series of 'What if?' questions to allow discussion of and preparation for unwanted or unexpected occurrences. For instance:

- What if the managing director/chief executive were to die suddenly?
- What if the MD received a tempting offer and left suddenly?

- What if the MD received a serious diagnosis of illness, requiring long-term treatment and rehabilitation?
- What if the main successor-in-waiting decides to leave the company?

The Succession Plan

As succession planning can be challenging, it is best to approach it in a methodical fashion, compiling a list of key questions, the answers to which will form the basis of the draft succession plan. The plan will need to balance the needs of the current owner, the next generation, the business and the wider family. The aim is to create a plan that is as fair as possible.

This succession plan is a stand-alone document that is agreed by the succession steering committee (a group charged with rolling out the succession – succession steering committees are discussed in more detail later in this chapter) and circulated only to them.

It is advisable to bring in an external advisor to help discuss and draft the succession plan. Throughout the succession process, it is important to seek expert professional advice, particularly on taxation, as there are various implications for those relinquishing ownership, control and management in terms of both business and personal finance. In fact, it is on issues of succession that external advisors usually work with a family business, more so than on any other process. There are various types of advisor that might be useful in this process: a bank manager can ensure that funds are available to effect share transfer; while an estate planner will take a long-term view and ensure that the transfer minimises tax consequences and incorporates features for future generations.

The role of the external advisor in this process is to coach the client to solve problems themselves through sharing their knowledge and experience, and teasing out the issues thrown up by the succession debate. He or she will also help during the actual transition, offering support, advice and helping the client to stay on track with the plan they have decided upon. The most effective approach is for the outgoing managing director and management team to work alongside a team of complementary advisors to create and implement the succession plan.

The Key Elements of a Succession Plan

There is much to consider before drafting a succession plan, but essentially, the succession plan should set out the following:

- WHAT the owner intends to do, and WHY.
- WHO the owner intends to pass the business on to.
- HOW the owner intends to manage the transition process.
- WHEN the owner intends to make the transition and start relinquishing control.

WHAT the owner intends to do, and WHY

First, consideration should be given to both of the following:

1. Transfer of ownership.
2. Transfer of leadership or management.

Day-to-day management of a business, which enables it to operate effectively, and the ownership of its shares are two distinct issues, meaning that the roles of shareholders and managers are distinct and therefore must be treated differently. For instance, sometimes the family will continue to own the business after its founder or owner/manager leaves, opting to be shareholders, rather than managers, while management might be passed on to a key non-family board member. Alternatively, a junior family member may take a controlling stake and become the new CEO when the existing CEO leaves. Therefore, in terms of a transfer of ownership, current owners should consider who will own stock once they have stepped down.

With regard to the transfer of leadership, the current leader of the family business (probably the founder) needs to consider who will **lead and manage** the business once he or she has stepped down.

According to an MGI survey on family and private business,[1] **continuity** is a key requirement in sustaining success in business. Maintaining control of ownership, providing liquidity for family owners to exit, securing sufficient capital for growth and adequately funding retirement all loom large as major challenges to continuity – as does selecting an ownership structure for the following generation, selecting the right leader and enabling shared family control.

---

[1] Dana, L.E. and Smyrnios, K.X., "From the Family Room to the Board Room: Family Business in Focus" (MGI, 2010).

To enable continuity while simultaneously meeting the owner's needs, succession requirements should be considered in light of the following questions:

- Is *succession* (to a family or non-family member) the best course of action for the business and the family? Or would a trade sale or management buy-out or other alternative exit strategy be more viable? Are funds needed to finance the owner's retirement? What are the pros and cons of each option?
- What are your core objectives and main goals for the succession process? For example, to ensure the future success of the business once you are gone or to make the transition process as smooth as possible?
- If you intend to pass the business on, why is that so important to you? What role would you want to play in the next-generation business, if any?
- What will you *do* about ownership and leadership succession? What will the ownership structure look like? Will you nominate and select a successor? Develop a process for shared family control? Will ownership be passed on to your spouse or your children? Or might successors only assume the role of shareholders, with seats on the board, and leave the role of leadership and management to key non-family executives, effectively sharing control?
- Will you pass ownership and leadership control to one main family leader? Or will this be passed on to a team of siblings (and more passive shareholders)?
- What will be done about the equitable division of shares? Will you divide shares and transfer equity equally, rewarding both active and passive members? Or will you distribute shares on the basis of involvement, contribution and participation in the business and differentiate between active and passive members?[2]

---

[2] Note: one way to address the issue of 'passive' family members preventing active family members from leading effectively is to recapitalise the shareholding structure to create two classes of share (voting and non-voting). This enables active family members with adequate control to have agility when making decisions without being hampered by passive family members (as they are unable to vote) and yet enables the owner-manager to distribute ownership more equally between their children.

- Who will be included in the decision-making process? What will be the key criteria that the intended successor must meet? How will that decision be confirmed and communicated?
- What are the responsibilities and rights of shareholders? Is the upcoming generation aware of and prepared to take those on?
- What is your Plan B, in case Plan A doesn't work out? For example, if your chosen successor declines or moves abroad or you need to reconsider policy about family member leaders.

WHO the owner intends to pass the business on to

Again, there are many questions and options to consider when drafting a plan deciding on the next owner of the business:

- Does the next generation wish to own shares in the business? How active or passive are they currently in terms of their involvement in the business?
- Is there an obvious choice of successor within the family?
- Is that natural successor ready? Or do they need to be developed and prepared to step up to take on the leadership role?
- If there isn't a single obvious successor, who are the most likely candidates?
- Are those on the successor shortlist able to demonstrate commitment, appropriate credentials, track record, skills and capabilities? Do they share the company's vision and values?
- What qualifications, credentials, experience and skills should the successor have?
- Might an external appointment be necessary?
- Is shared leadership an option?
- Might key non-family employees take shares or will they be put into a trust?
- Has it been agreed (and stipulated in your family constitution) that there should always be a family member/leader on the board?
- Would it be preferable to let a non-family CEO take the helm while family members remain on the board and continue to own voting shares?
- Will there be an interim leader in the meantime or will the current leader gradually pass over responsibilities until the transition date?
- How might you deal with potential resentment from family members who see themselves as being overlooked?

- Should an internal or external non-family member take over as leader?
- How will you communicate your decision and make it clear that your choice is in the best interests of the business?

Arriving at a final decision on the successor might be very obvious and straightforward, or it might be an extremely difficult call to make. There might be more than one obvious choice for successor. It could be that there are three or more entirely capable potential leaders all ready and willing to step up and take the helm. How does an owner choose between his or her own children?

EXAMPLE: DARLEY – LETTING THE CHILDREN DECIDE[3]

One answer is to pass that decision over to the generation in question and let them decide. That's what US-based firefighting equipment firm Darley did when its founder decided to step down in 1995. The firm enjoyed an annual turnover of $170 million, so it was imperative it be left in a safe pair of hands, to ensure the future of the business and the family's wealth. Darley had considered a shared or rotating presidency, so that each of the three possible successors could take turns, but the outgoing CEO (the successors' father) opted instead to make his three sons decide between themselves. So they each submitted business plans and the three of them collaborated on the final decision. The process took five years, until finally, due to his commendable communication and organisational skills and detailed, passionate business plan, two of the brothers put their support behind their other brother, Paul. They chose the most dedicated sibling who would be the best leader, who they knew would be fair, and with whom they shared the same values. The chosen president has the support of his siblings and the rest of the firm. The previous CEO's approach has proven solid, as the firm has since grown from strength to strength.

---

[3] Gardella, A., "Family Businesses Learn to Adapt to Keep Thriving", *New York Times*, 4 April 2012.

While it may seem unpalatable to some current owners to leave this vital decision in the hands of those who are applying for the role, it is important not to rush the decision and to involve as many people in the process as possible, so that the decision is well-informed and founded on consensus.

Recruiting a new managing director should be a robust and rigorous process, so it's worth seeking professional expert help. Regardless of whether the candidates are family members or non-family members, the following guidelines will help to design an application process that will secure the best candidate for the role:

- **Define the required competencies and outline key criteria**, i.e. prioritise must-have skills and experience.
- **Identify the most promising internal (or external) candidates** who have the potential to take on the role, and define in detail how the transition would be effected.
- **Set a transition timetable with the potential candidate(s)** – agree a fixed period within which the outgoing managing director will pass over control to the new one.
- **Test candidates in environments outside of their comfort zones** – evaluate how well they run day-to-day operations by setting specific tasks and tests.

CASE STUDY: M I DICKSON LTD – DECIDING ON A SUCCESSOR[4]

As featured in the M I Dickson case studies presented throughout the book, Michael Dickson provides interesting insights into the succession process in the family firm:

"Serious consideration of succession planning began about eight years ago. Truth be told, we had no plan, a phenomenon that seems to be the general rule in smaller family businesses. I suppose we're all reluctant to think too deeply about the future and our own mortality and tend to follow an assumption that life won't change and we're going to live forever, so

---

[4] Dickson, M., Interview with author (July 2013).

we refuse to contemplate any scenario other than the present. That inevitably leads to a reactive policy dictating future action, which seems a pretty limiting approach when you look at it in the cold light of day.

"Life does change in the most dramatic ways, and Christine's unexpected death could have resulted in far greater trauma, and perhaps even a forced sale, had we not put measures in place. Thankfully, with the support and steady encouragement of a specialist in the field, we were some way along the road when this tragedy befell us. Back in 2006, we didn't particularly want to sell the business and retire, but we also didn't feel that we could command a value that would reflect the business's contribution to family wealth or provide anything like the replacement capital needed to sustain current or projected earnings.

"Chris and I were having trouble thinking past that, but our specialist advisor suggested that many successful companies had not only survived, but grown significantly as enterprises while remaining family-owned but not necessarily family-run.

"Continuing family input would be required to appoint and set targets for an executive board and to ensure those targets were being met. It seemed the best mechanism to deliver that over the long term was via an inclusive family council. We then had to establish who would want to participate, other than my second daughter who was already working in the business. I was concerned that an approach from me would be seen as overt pressure, so our advisor offered to speak with the five bloodline beneficiaries under our will trusts.

"I need not have worried – all expressed their pride and interest in the family firm and willingness to form a family council. It's now been going for over four years. The chair is elected by the family members and we have a constitution that, while not legally binding, we've all signed up to as a reflection of our common intent. Our company articles were changed to reflect the aims of the constitution so that only bloodline family members may hold shares and we set up a discretionary trust to receive the current shares on the death of shareholders.

"As I said, the council meets biannually, where I make a formal presentation as MD and members receive monthly accounts and a detailed activity report. The family council chair and I have a monthly telephone discussion and update which is then disseminated to the group. In parallel with the establishment of the council, we made various operational changes and some appointments which reflected the growth of the business and also acknowledged the need for a succession strategy. We moved from quarterly to monthly accounting, appointed a financial controller and a cost accountant. We also appointed a commercial manager in 2012, whose activities have recently been complemented with a further commercial appointment; a general manager now leads our production facility and a head of retail has been appointed to drive growth and new product development in the retail business.

"In 2012 we appointed our first external, non-executive director and a new team of external accountants. The managing partner of the accountancy practice contributes at quarterly board meetings, as does our family council chair (currently our eldest son and NED) along with our second daughter, who has worked in the business for 10 years and was recently elected an executive director.

"These changes may not seem particularly surprising if viewed from the perspective of a non-family business background. However, we grew organically with virtually no external input as a sort of benevolent dictatorship, where decisions could be taken on a whim and the idea of business planning and budgets were foreign concepts ... so they've made a significant impact on the way we think and act. The changes required a clear commitment to the future; we had to visualise a future in which we had no input, and that was quite a challenge for us.

"We weren't anticipating Christine becoming ill, but we were anticipating her retirement and could have found ourselves in a much darker place but for the persistence and tenacity of our succession planning advisor. When I speak to friends and acquaintances in the family business sector I often despair at their lack of appetite to deal with these very same issues.

"To be family-owned but not necessarily family-run seems to be the most realistic approach to guaranteeing the survival of the company and preserving the family's wealth. When I do retire from operational matters in the next couple of years, my daughter will be the only operational family executive in the business.

"Time will tell whether she or the heads of production and retail will step up to replace me as MD, but whatever happens in that regard and whatever their ambitions turn out to be, the presence of a Dickson family director and its resonance with our employees and customers cannot be underestimated. We lose that continuity at our peril and I see that as the next challenge along the road."

Certainly the wheels are in motion for succession, as changes have already been made in a gradual process to reduce owner dependency and prepare talented employees of the firm to take on more responsibility. This makes it easier for Michael to envisage a future outside of the business. The unfortunate death of his sister, Christine, provided a strong reminder of the unpredictability of life and that succession planning should not be left too late.

HOW the owner intends to manage the transition process

Some family business owners wish to treat all of their children fairly and see giving each of them an equal share in the business as the only way to do that. However, this is not always the fairest course of action because not all of them may be contributing to the business equally.

For instance, suppose a family has four children: two siblings are working in the family business; the other two have separate careers and no involvement or interest in the family firm. It would be unfair for each of the four siblings to be given the same equal share in the business because those working in the company deserve to be recognised and rewarded for their efforts.

So, how can there be equality with estate planning in such a situation?

First, it's important to be very clear on what fairness means, and that it is more important than equality. It's also advisable to seek external advice and let the advisors present to the board or steering group. The three main components of ownership change then need to be considered:

1. Control
2. Income
3. Retained earnings and dividend policy

It is worth considering each of these components separately, depending on the objectives and needs of the business and the family.

Control

Control in this context refers to the ownership of voting shares. Shares can have voting or non-voting rights. In passing control, the owner may decide that the children who work in the business could be given voting shares and thus control the business (and keeping the decision-making power with those who understand the business), while the children who do not work in the business are given ordinary non-voting shares. Because they own shares, all children could earn dividends and all would benefit if the company were sold.

Another option would be to pass on ownership control (i.e. 51% or more of the voting shares) to one child. This would mean that an agreement amongst the siblings would not be required to make strategic decisions for the company, as the majority shareholder would ultimately control the company. However, this could cause other problems within a family.

There are certainly many options and these should be discussed and worked out in order to reach a way of dividing up the estate so that everyone is treated fairly. In most cultures, parents are inclined to treat their children equally in terms of value of the gift or inheritance.

Income

Family members who work in the business will receive their salary for their role in the business and the two roles of ownership and management need to be seen as separate. The only way family members who do not work in the business receive an income from the business is by means of a dividend.

Retained Earnings and Dividend Policy

It is important to have a policy on retained earnings and dividends. Shareholders will want a return on their investment/shareholding paid annually by means of a dividend. This is particularly important for the shareholders who do not work in the business. Retained earnings are necessary for the business to grow and not all profits will be paid out by means of a dividend. Any undistributed profits are available for future draw-down, will strengthen the balance sheet and are for the benefit of all shareholders.

As with everything else to do with succession planning, there are many options regarding how the process is rolled out. For example, the departing MD might not retire completely but stagger retirement by retaining a seat on the board or moving up to be chairman (in charge of the board) or take an NED role before leaving the firm completely. It's important to remember that succession is a journey that takes time and should not be rushed.

In preparing for drafting the final succession plan, the succession steering group should sketch out a picture of what everything should look like once the business transfer has been completed, taking into consideration:

- the financial profile of the retiring owner;
- how the business will be governed post-succession;
- how the financial stability of the enterprise can be best assured;
- any specific provisions that need to be made for future generations that may eventually own company stock; and
- any specific plans that must be made to effect the full and complete transfer to the successor.

WHEN the owner intends to make the transition and start relinquishing control

As well as being clear on how to make the transition a success, it is also necessary to figure out *when* best to take each step towards transition and beyond. Accordingly, a schedule of clear deadlines or milestones can be appended to the succession plan. This enables detailed preparation on all sides, helps the current owner to start disconnecting from the business and allows the next generation to move confidently into their new positions.

When compiling such a timetable, consider the following:

- Is there an ideal time for a succession or sale (if there is no successor) to take place? The timing comes down to the length of preparation required, the stage that individuals are at in their lives (both the current leader and the next) and so on. According to Ivan Lansberg, "Succession is driven by a biological clock. The ages of the senior leaders of the business and of their designated successors determine the timing of the succession."[5]
- Should there be a compulsory retirement age or should it depend on various circumstances, as outlined in the succession plan?

TIPS FOR SUCCESSFUL SUCCESSION PLANNING

- To ensure that succession planning is effective, transparent and fair, the process should include as much dialogue as possible.

- An effective precursor to the whole process is to clarify the vision of where the business is going and synchronise that vision with the skills and competencies of family members.

- Draw an organogram (a diagram or plan that gives the names and job titles of all the staff in an organisation, showing how they are connected to each other) of what the business might look like after the owner has left. This is something Michael Dickson of M I Dickson found useful: "The family council set me a task of describing what the organogram of the business would look like that would replace me. I took that very seriously, because how could I ask them for ongoing engagement if I didn't?" Drawing the new make-up of the company in this way can focus on the mind on the best solutions to the various questions posed by succession.

[5] Lansberg, I., *Succeeding Generations* (Harvard Business Review Press, 1999).

- Enable the outgoing MD to step back progressively, rather than step down. This might mean him or her gradually relinquishing control as MD and becoming chairman, non-executive director, or taking on a separate role for the company's charitable foundation, if it has one.

- Open a dialogue early on with the next generation. (See **Chapter 8** for more on how to effectively engage the next generation.)

- Empower the next generation. Do this by coaching and developing, supporting and implementing ideas. Make them feel ready to assume the leadership.

- Communicate the proposed changes and new vision in good time. Staff, customers and suppliers should all be kept informed about the current owner's plans to cease involvement and who is taking over the reins and why he or she is the perfect candidate for the job. This is all about maintaining relationships and credibility and preventing key stakeholders from losing faith in the business as a result of the transition to a new leader or owner.

2. Preparation

After planning, preparation is the second key ingredient to ensuring success when it comes to succession. There are a number of areas that must be tackled in this regard:

- The feelings, concerns and mindset of the outgoing leader.
- Reducing owner dependency.
- Developing the new leader or leaders.
- Establishing a succession steering committee.

The Feelings, Concerns and Mindset of the Outgoing Leader

There is a wide spectrum of reactions and expectations to manage when succession is under discussion, not least those of the current owner. Stepping aside or down is never straightforward. It represents the end of an era, a way of life, and the owner's feelings on this will change over time, but will usually be intensely felt. It is important for the owner, as well as staff and family members, to recognise this.

If you are an owner, it is quite normal for talk of succession and planning to make you feel anxious. You are facing into a largely unknown future, a perhaps unwelcome retirement life and there is a multitude of issues that must be addressed and resolved before you can move on. It's challenging and daunting, although hopefully also exciting to some degree. The key thing to understand, however, is that hanging on is dangerous. The business can suffer if you refuse to let go. The consequences are not what you would want for the business you have worked so hard to build:

- **The most competent successors leave and the worst stay as they have no other option.** The best talent and most likely successors with the most potential could leave due to frustration and becoming bored at the lack of challenge or reward for their hard work. It would be a huge loss to the business to waste their ideas, energy and commitment.
- **Family relationships are adversely affected.** The ignored next generation, who are not delegated to or trusted with more responsibility, get angry and feel alienated and resentful. They feel they are still being treated as children when they are grown adults who are more than capable, especially if you give them the chance to prove themselves.
- **The business suffers financially.** Morale declines, strategies stagnate and skilful people leave. There is less innovation, energy and drive as the younger generation becomes alienated.

If, as an owner, you are struggling to let go, there are things you can do to lessen those negative feelings:

- **Reward your work.** Outgoing MDs should be generous to themselves. After all, they've worked long and hard to afford the next generation this opportunity and they should reap the benefits.
- **Disassociate from the business.** Develop an identity outside of the business. Joining other boards involved in charity work or joining a business mentoring program to lend expertise to start-ups could be considered.
- **Retire *to* something rather than *from* something.** What can you focus on? Something new to learn? Something else to lead,

whether that's a charitable foundation, local trade association or club? In order to achieve well-being in life beyond work, we need to do things that make our lives meaningful and partake in activities that engage us. If you can discover what those engaging activities and meaningful purposes are before you leave the business, you'll find it far easier to let go.

- **Take a staggered approach towards retirement to make it easier to bear.** As suggested above, become chairman and/or an NED. Alter your remit from running the company to running the board, so strategy is the focus more than operations.
- **Talk!** All of these fears, concerns and worries should be openly discussed among all generations involved, with external advisors helping to guide discussions if necessary. Dialogue – talking and listening – is as vital as planning when it comes to succession and exit.

Part of the mindset of letting go is, of course, handing over. Often it is not the letting go that causes trouble, it's the thought of a son or daughter becoming 'the boss', and fears surrounding their ability to succeed. For owners struggling with this aspect, some guiding advice:

- **Focus on the shared vision and common goal,** i.e. for the business to continue and succeed. In order for this to happen, the strengths of each family member need to be brought into play.
- **Let your children grow up and have faith in them.** You've brought your children up well, they have learned from you and they are eager to prove themselves. Remember to enjoy their progress and applaud it.

Owners who run family businesses with strong values, vision and stewardship will tend to hand over control and voting stock to their successors early and step back to become chairmen. This creates an environment of mutual respect. These businesses act decisively and don't wait for the MD to lose stamina and focus or for the business to lose competitive advantage or talented people.

By stepping back gradually into a chairman or non-executive role, the owner can let go gradually at a pace that suits them and, importantly, the company as well. Of course, chairman is not just an honorary role; it requires staying up to speed with what's going on and it's a lot of responsibility to ensure that the board properly evaluates executive performance, communicates effectively with shareholders, protects the company's assets and fulfils its legal and compliance obligations.

Reducing Owner Dependency

Owner dependency can work both ways: an owner who is too dependent on the business; or a business that fears losing its owner.

An owner who is reluctant to leave can generate much negative feeling among the next generation, who often interpret this reluctance as a comment on their abilities. For the next generation, it's important to be aware of the possible reasons behind the owner's reluctance. They could be worrying about:

- **Readiness and abilities of the next generation.** Will they be able to successfully lead the company that the owner/owners have worked so hard to build? Does leaving mean overburdening young shoulders?
- **Choosing between their children.** There is normally a desire to be fair and equitable, and to try to ensure that nobody's feelings are hurt by the choice of successor.
- **Their own role and identity post-handover.** The business has been their life – what will they do now that they are retiring? Will they lose their identity and prestige now that they have relinquished control of their business? How will their spouse cope with them at home? How will they stay in touch with business colleagues and friends?
- **Their own mortality.** Having heard stories about people retiring and becoming ill or even dying within months, they fear that if they stop this will also happen to them.
- **Not being able to afford to retire** and not wishing to use resources from the business to do so comfortably.

As a result of these worries, and particularly if they remain unexpressed, an owner can stay in the business too long – either as MD, or on the fringes, constantly tinkering with whatever they can get their hands on. According to Gerard Burke, co-author of *Growing Your Business: A Handbook for Ambitious Owner-managers*:

"Many owner-managers fall into the trap of becoming what we call the 'meddler' because these people that they have employed, of course, don't do things quite the same way as the original owner-manager did and by definition therefore, it's probably wrong..."[6]

While the well-intended wish of the owner-manager is to make the business successful, interference can be hugely detrimental. Good leaders spot and unlock potential, build confidence, cultivate skills and motivate. Conversely, meddling undermines confidence, stifles skills and demoralises. Meddlers prevent people from proving their worth. By passing on non-mission critical tasks gradually to others and delegating responsibilities, the business is more likely to flourish because the MD can focus on its growth rather than day-to-day operations.

"The hardest thing for many owner-managers to take on board is an acceptance that they will contribute *more* by doing *less*," comments David Molian, Gerard Burke's co-author.

There are practical steps that can help an owner-manager to prepare for the moment of departure in the most effective way possible:

- **Set a firm cut-off point and retirement date**, otherwise the MD may think, "Just one more deal to make", "Just a bit more to add to the retirement pot". A clearly defined timeline for retirement helps avoid the common problem of the MD dragging out the process and gives them adequate time to prepare.
- **Develop the successor sufficiently ahead of the transition date.** The departing MD will feel far more confident leaving the business in capable hands, and the incoming MD will feel more confident in taking the business on.
- **Move from being accountable to being accountable for making sure *others* are accountable.** That way you are still involved, but at arm's length.
- **Play a supportive role before leaving.** Support new strategies that the successor wishes to implement before the departure date.
- **Stick to the plan.** This is good advice from Patrick Buckley, Deputy MD at EPS Group (see case study below), in describing the company's transition from first to second generation: "There was an agreed process, there was a plan, everyone set their date,

---

[6] Burke, G. *et al.*, *Growing Your Business: A Handbook for Ambitious Owner-managers* (Routledge, 2008).

and the process was put in place as to who would step up and take responsibility once each owner/manager/director retired and we just followed that process. In total seven owners, directors and senior managers will have retired during the period 2008–2014."

- **Create new roles for seniors**, such as company 'ambassadors', whereby the younger generation, while managing the day-to-day business, can continue to benefit from their experience when needed.
- **Avoid interfering with or undermining the new MD.** Enable them to have the freedom to do things their way. If you are still involved and are gradually stepping back, hold meetings with the new MD offsite. Meddling is not helpful.
- **Keep a low profile.** Provide new and existing managers with the knowledge, tools and authority to do the job while you begin to have a lower profile. Gradually transfer this knowledge while you, for example, work from home to keep a lower profile.
- **Focus on building a solid and successful organisation.** Establish clear communication, clear decision-making processes, as well as good governance, so that the business can prosper without you. In this way you will have left your stamp on the business and laid strong foundations.
- **Implement the transition slowly but surely, step by step.** The gradual transfer of decision-making power will help the new generation adapt to their new roles and responsibilities more smoothly than if the process is rushed or sudden.

The Successor

So far, we have focused on the departing owner in terms of reducing dependency, but is there anything the successor can do to help as well? Founders are a hard act to follow. While the outgoing MD has to deal with their own concerns, the incoming MD will also have issues to address. He or she might be questioning if this is the right career choice, if it's possible to live up to the owner's expectations and if the staff will react positively to their appointment. For the successor, this can be a difficult transition, and he or she would be wise to:

- Create forums where family and non-family members can share their concerns, where ideas and thoughts and communication

are focused, so that they can stay in the loop and hear what everyone is saying.
- Spend time learning from and being mentored by the predecessor, in order to gain the benefit of their knowledge and experience.

Developing the New Leader or Leaders

A good way for an owner-manager to move on from a business is to focus on being a leader rather than an owner. This encourages a mental shift away from the day-to-day operations to the long-term stability and profitability of the company.

In order to become a better leader and develop new leaders within and for the business:

- **Encourage proactive thinking** and ask managers what *they* would do.
- **Empower the people you have chosen and build trust through delegating responsibilities.** As long as you've been clear about expectations, trust that the right decisions will be made.
- **Develop leaders who can deliver** and exceed expectations by gradually passing on more and more responsibility and handing over the operational reins.
- **Give your potential successor(s) some space.** Take time away from the office to meet partners, customers and creatively strategize.
- **Focus on directing the company's future** instead of directing staff.

Establishing a Succession Steering Committee

It is advisable to set up a **steering committee** to plan, prepare and ultimately implement the succession process. This creates a sense of the succession being an important event for the company, not just for the individuals involved. The committee could be made up of a mixture of board and family council members, as well as non-management or retired family members, along with an external advisor if possible. No potential succession candidates should be part of the committee, as the committee needs to be independent.

The role of the committee should be to provide steady guidance throughout the change process, as well as monitoring commitment, compliance and the pace of the transition. It should:

- assess the impact change may have within the business and family, and address how to guide everyone through those changes;
- ensure that everyone involved in the preparation and selection of the successor is adequately prepared;
- consider the timing of succession announcements;
- monitor the departing MD's behaviour in terms of letting go;
- evaluate the candidates' capabilities;
- provide counsel for both the outgoing and incoming MDs;
- mentor the successor so that he or she can successfully articulate his or her vision, goals and strategy for the business; and
- keep other family members informed.

The steering committee will probably stay operational up to a year after the successor has taken over to ensure that change is well-managed, all parties are coping well and that the impact on the business and its growth is a positive one.

SUMMARY OF GUIDELINES FOR OWNERS FOR EFFECTIVE TRANSITION MANAGEMENT AND SUCCESSION PREPARATION

- **Equip your successor sufficiently.** Pass on your knowledge, experience, methods and vision through training sessions and mentoring.

- **Empower the next generation.** Give them the opportunity to be involved in the decision-making process long before they take control. Step back in stages. Start to give them responsibility for making important decisions so they will learn how to weigh up pros and cons and reach the right decision for the company.

- **Test their readiness at regular intervals** so you can gradually reduce your involvement.

- **Include in the succession plan a development plan for 'candidates in waiting'** so that they are adequately groomed and nobody is expected to take a 'leap of faith'. This might include bringing one or more candidates to work underneath the current owner-manager for a year, so they have the opportunity to prove themselves before the reigns are handed over.

This grooming period would result in more of the day-to-day work being gradually handed over until there is mutual confidence in the successor's ability to take on the role.

- **Provide a mentor/coach for those candidates.** Give them a sounding board and help prepare them for the role.

- **Enable your candidates to implement and enforce ideas.** Give them ownership of projects, areas of the business, key decisions, etc., before they take on full company ownership or management. This gives you a chance to assess their leadership and management skills in practice and to gain confidence in their ideas.

- **Invite candidates to board meetings** to present on how they might boost company efficiency and which strategic growth plans they might pursue. Exposure to the board before they take charge is vital.

- **Draft your own plan of what the future could look like.** This could include growth and reinvestment strategies, talent recruitment and retention goals, tips on motivating future generations to get involved, succession guidance and a clear vision and values statement. The successor(s) may choose to use this road map to set their direction, they may use some of it but tweak parts of it to suit their fresh ideas and new objectives, or they might ignore it completely. Yet writing this plan and passing it on to your successors will help you feel that you've done all you can and be confident that the business is now in safe hands.

A Tale of Two Families

To conclude this chapter, I shall illustrate the points discussed through two contrasting case studies, exploring the experiences of the Taylor and Buckley families. In the first case study, we will see how the Taylor family handles succession badly and its adverse effects on their business. In the second case study, the Buckley family shows how to implement a succession plan correctly. There are lessons to be learned from finding out how successful families have managed the challenges of family dynamics, and there are sobering lessons to be learned from the families who have failed and allowed a once thriving business to collapse.

Case Study 1: The Taylor Family – Poor Planning, Poor Preparation, Poor Transition Management

Terry Taylor left school at the age of 14 and went to work in a provincial drapery store. He worked hard, had a good way with customers and impressed his employer. He attended the local technical school at night, studying bookkeeping and commerce. His boss was keen to retain his service and offered him a permanent position with improved wages. But Terry wanted to broaden his horizons.

He applied for and took up a better position in a bigger company in a nearby town. This was just the first in a series of moves at decent intervals, each move an improvement on the previous one. He eventually became a commercial traveller for a well-known firm of men's outfitters. He quickly became their top salesman, with a high salary and good commission. He enjoyed working for the company and loved his job, but his ambition was driving him to greater heights.

He had been earning good money for a number of years and had been smart enough to save rather than spend. Terry sought a meeting with his local bank manager and discussed his plans to set up in business for himself in a busy location in Dublin. His timing was excellent, business was brisk and he ploughed every penny back into the business. He married, raised a family and opened more shops. By the early 1960s, he had 10 shops in Dublin and the provinces, all well located. The business was very profitable and Terry enjoyed a high standard of living. He had four sons and four daughters and all were encouraged to get a university education.

The boys were encouraged to pursue business courses and the girls were steered towards liberal arts courses. Terry never made any secret of his aims. He was building the business for the boys; the girls would be well educated and hopefully well married with a good "dowry". There was never any attempt to attract the daughters to the business. The boys, with the exception of Jack, Terry's eldest son, completed their degrees or professional qualifications and came directly into the business. Jack completed his degree and Terry succeeded in placing him with a friendly supplier, so that he could get practical experience. Jack wasn't too happy with this arrangement and always claimed he was anxious to "roll up his sleeves and get stuck into the family business".

The boys were still quite young and immature. Terry, while being a hard grafter and very dynamic, also had a very forceful personality. He was conscious that he was a fairly wealthy man and he was determined that he was not going to pay any "estate duty" on his wealth. At that time, if a person gifted his estate to his children and survived for seven years, estate duty could be avoided. So while his sons were still relatively young and immature, he transferred all the shares in his business to them, in the process making them very wealthy young men. They were over-confident in their own abilities and reluctant to listen to the advice of experienced advisors. They retired "the old man" and took full charge of the running and development of the company. They undertook to pay the founder a pension out of the firm's funds; no arrangements were made for an independent fund.

Within a short period they had doubled the number of outlets, but unfortunately had been less selective than their father in picking the locations. The net result was that not only were these new outlets not profitable but they were a considerable drain on the existing profitable stores. To equip and stock this expansion programme meant substantial borrowings. Borrowings cost money and borrowed money has to be repaid. It can be difficult to meet repayment commitments if the firm is losing money.

These young men had been brought up in very comfortable circumstances and wanted to continue that lifestyle. In due course they got married, bought fine houses, drove big cars, and lived the good life.

However, the business was unable to sustain their lifestyles. As regularly happens in tough trading times, they started squabbling and blaming each other for the poor trading results. Instead of fighting the market, they were fighting each other. It was pointless to prolong the agony – the company was eventually put into liquidation with a very substantial deficit.

Reasons for the Failure

- **Inability to pass on the vision.** Either the founder failed to pass on his vision or his sons were unable to correctly interpret it and reshape it to meet the demands of changing times.
- **Lack of expectation management causing a feeling of entitlement.** The sons believed that, as Taylors, they were entitled to management roles in their business, even though, with one half-hearted exception, they did not adequately prepare themselves for the managerial roles they were given. Degrees and qualifications are all very well, but they must be grounded in practical training and experience.
- **No conflict resolution procedures were in place.** The family wasted a lot of time squabbling rather than devising strategy or being productive and there were no procedures in place to achieve resolution.
- **Failure to professionalise the business.** There was no attempt to professionalise the business (see **Chapter 7**), nor did they have a strategic plan. Meetings were ad hoc and decisions were not recorded. Communication between the brothers was poor. There were no formal board meetings and no consideration given to the appointment of independent non-executive directors.
- **No board, therefore no exit strategy.** If there had been an effective board, the sons would have been replaced by professional managers or a decision would have been made to sell the business. Sadly, this did not happen and the business continued until the money ran out and it was forced into liquidation.

CASE STUDY 2: THE BUCKLEY FAMILY AND THE EPS GROUP –
GOOD VISION, GOOD STRATEGY, GOOD TRANSITION[7]

The family's original business, Kanturk Electrical and Farm Services Ltd, was founded in 1968 by Gerald Buckley and his friend, J Sheehan. EPS (Electrical & Pump Services) was founded a number of years later by Gerald with his brother, Paddy. His other brother, Tadhg, and sister, Betty, joined the business in the mid-1970s. The first generation of four siblings grew the business well together. Today, the second generation consists of 17, eight of whom work in the business (or 47% of the second generation). Patrick Buckley, the current deputy MD and son of Gerald, takes up the story:

"The company started off very early on as a small business. It was very much a team effort and everyone got stuck in and played their part in developing the business. There were a lot of non-family members in the business, both at management level and employee level, who have contributed to the success of the company over the years. And so the business progressed along.

"Initially it was a products business before expanding into services and eventually into joint ventures and strategic alliances. In the early 1980s, the business became heavily involved in water and wastewater treatment and a number of strategic acquisitions and partnerships took place. The first generation of siblings developed the business gradually across a number of platforms and now, with the help of the second generation, the firm has extended and diversified the business. The first generation of the company had always focused on water, wastewater treatment and pumping. The second generation have made a big impact over the last five years, growing the company in Ireland, the UK and elsewhere."

The business is currently at the final stage of the transition from the first to second generation (which is made up of siblings

---

[7] Buckley, P., Interview with author (July 2013).

and cousins), with the majority of the eight second-generation members having worked in the company for many years.

"Some started straight into the business," says Patrick, who himself joined the company in 1997 full-time as his first job after university. He joined the board in 2008. "Others have gone off and pursued careers elsewhere and then joined the business at other stages, so there's a mixture and balance.

"The founding fathers have all left bar one: Tadgh Buckley, our current MD and chairperson, retires in 2014.

"We're already delivering our plan and we're expanding the business in the UK and in Ireland. One of our biggest customers in Ireland is the local authority sector – there have been some big changes in Ireland with the formation of Irish Water, so that throws up a big challenge for the business but also a lot of opportunities. It's a very exciting time to be involved in water and for us it's just to continue doing what we do well and improving that, but also being mindful of the changes in our market and making sure that we position the business to make the most of those opportunities.

"I've never worked in a non-family business, so I can't compare. But for me personally working in a family business *is* the sense of achievement. There's a sense of the ability to take something that is successful and turn it into something that's more successful; to take something that was started from scratch in 1968, developed and managed and grown by an exceptional group of people who made some very strategic decisions in growing the business in very difficult times. Over 33 years they developed an excellent business and the second generation of family and non-family have worked alongside them for the last 15 to 20 years. So we've been part of the recent growth and now our challenge is to take it forward.

"One of the models that a lot of successful family businesses use is that you would have to go off and spend a minimum of five to 10 years proving yourself in another business before you would be invited to join the family business."

Each of the family members in the second generation worked from an early age in the business, generally over the summer holidays. "We were no different than any other employee: we would have been grafting in different parts of the business and learning from there."

"The company now has a new board, which is made up of a good mix of family and non-family members with a diverse and dynamic mix of expertise and skill sets. This provides a good, challenging and dynamic environment that ensures you can expect the best possible outcome for any business decision."

The company is currently focused on the Irish, UK and Middle East markets and has a strong balance sheet of €23 million. As the company continues to grow and the final first-generation member is set to retire, the pride, passion and shared vision of the second generation shines through as they take control and steer this sustainable and successful company to even greater heights.

Reasons for the Success of the Buckley Family/EPS Group

- **Clarity of shared vision and strategy.** "We have a lot of clarity around what we're about and what our vision is going forward whilst the business is moving from first to second generation," says Patrick. "We want to ensure that we have a shared, collective vision that will take the business forward so that everyone knows where they figure in the process."
- **Role clarity.** "Our roles depend on age, experience to date, career development, education and aptitude and the way you adapt yourself to the business model that we currently pursue. Everybody had their own preferences for what they wanted to do in college or post-secondary, so that would have set the scene for what we all do in the business."
- **A clear and well-considered, long-term succession plan.** "The company agreed its succession plan in 2007. It began in 2008 and will end in 2014. It's all laid out in terms of what will happen when which person retires in which year. A lot of the people who were promoted to new management roles

have worked alongside and for the original management team for the last 15 to 20 years, so it's a seamless transition. You definitely need to have a very clear and workable plan."

- **A well-selected team of external advisors.** "You very much need to carefully select your advisors in terms of legal, tax and people management concerns; it's very important to have an outside view of the process. You do need external advice from someone who understands the company, the people and the dynamic."

- **A non-family member to manage the succession process.** "We identified a non-family member to lead the process in terms of the coordination and linkages between the shareholders, the first and second generation family and the non-family employees, attending to the shareholding structure (ownership) of the company. The non-family members of the board are kept up to speed on the transition process and some of them are involved in that process. There are no secret family meetings: it's all above board, and everyone at board level is a key part of the development. This hopefully trickles down to rest of the team – everyone is kept in the loop."

- **A clear timetable of actions and a clear structure on feedback process.** "If you issue a number of shareholding blocks as we have, you need to identify a leader of each block so that you can coordinate the process of feedback from each block and also have that link for the retired owner with the business operations. You need to put a timescale on it, and it needs to have dates and deadlines and be moving on in a timely fashion. But you also need to allow enough time for each individual shareholding block to come to their own decisions."

- **Clear and transparent guidelines and rules around roles and remuneration.** "There needs to be a clear distinction between being a family member and being an employee so that there is no confusion. Family members who do not work in the business are not entitled to be remunerated. You need clear guidelines and clear rules and structures around roles and remuneration in order to be transparent. All employees (family and non-family) should be paid market rate."

- **A formal structure/process for succession for future generations.** "As this is our first transition from first generation to the second, the challenge for us is to put a more formal structure in place around the succession process going forward so that in 10 or 15 years' time, when the third generation start to show interest, there's a proven process there for them to follow."

This chapter has explored in detail the planning, preparation and enactment of succession. It is a complex area for any family business to navigate, but the information and advice given here should set owners and successors-in-waiting on the right track. The first step must be an open and honest discussion about the issues, followed by the hard work necessary to draft a carefully considered and workable succession plan. The focus of this chapter has therefore been on preparing for the retirement of one generation and planning the advancement of the next.

This is not the only option for the family business, of course. In **Chapter 11**, we will examine the option of selling and how to optimise that process for the business and the family.

Exit Strategy: Selling the Business

Introduction

The decision to sell a family business usually stems from one of two causes:

1. There is no successor willing (or able) to take on the business.
2. The founder started the business with the intention of eventually selling it.

In this second scenario, the entrepreneur may have aimed to create wealth for his or her family by growing a successful, profitable business and then selling it for a good price.

For some founders, of course, it is difficult to countenance the idea of building to sell – it seems counterintuitive to those who wish to create a legacy. However, circumstances may arise that make selling the best option for both the family and the business. A good example of this is the case of a bed retailing company called Dreams.

EXAMPLE: WHEN SELLING IS THE RIGHT OPTION[1]

The co-founders of Dreams, Mike and Carol Clare, sold their 180-strong chain of bed retailers in 2008 for over £200 million, 22 years after they founded the company. Their children were far too young to take on the business and the couple were worn out after working at full pelt for over two decades. Taken altogether, this made Mike keen to explore new challenges:

---

[1] Institute for Family Business, "Case Study – Family Business Challenges", www.ifb.org.uk.

"I felt I'd proved myself – my aim had been to build a successful enterprise and I'd definitely done that. But at the back of my mind I felt there was more to come. With the business growing and running smoothly, it seemed the right time to sell."

Mike stepped down as chairman and MD, but retained both a small shareholder stake and a non-executive role as president. This decision worked for him because the business remained his passion and he was keen to stay involved, albeit in "a small, advisory way".

"Selling was an emotional experience," admits Mike, "but staying connected has helped."

Your family is likely to benefit whether you keep or sell your business, and both are valid options for successful family business owners. It is important to note that, once selling the business becomes the preferred (or necessary) exit strategy, the new focus must be on preparing it for sale to well-targeted buyers by identifying the main traders in the industry who can add value by acquiring your business and maximising its value.

In order to achieve the best outcome during the exit phase, it makes sense to know who the potential buyers are and prepare the business to suit their needs.

The other important thing to remember is that when a business is sold it must be able to function independently of the owner. Businesses that are wholly dependent on the activities and performance of their owners are unlikely to attract a significant capital value on a sale. At the point of sale, the business should be able to run without the involvement of the owner, except where the owner is performing a line management role that can be filled through normal recruitment.

Ultimately, exit is the final chance for the owner and family to be rewarded for their efforts, to bring the vision to fruition and, potentially, to earn a family fortune. As such, it will often be the most important financial transaction in an entrepreneur's life. For this reason, it requires careful planning, a watertight exit plan and single-minded focus to secure the best outcome possible.

Preparing the Exit Plan

In the previous chapter we saw the importance of drafting a well-considered succession plan to effect the smooth transition to a new phase in the life of the business. The same advice applies to the exit strategy. It must be planned far in advance, consider all aspects and consequences, strive to be objective and for the good of the business, and it must incorporate solutions to various possible scenarios.

In order to start compiling an exit plan, it is best to start with some questions to establish the owner's motives, feelings and ambitions regarding the sale of the business. Shaping answers to concrete questions makes it easier to strip away the emotional layers and proceed with a clear, focused mind on the important and necessary issues. There are six key questions that will form the basis of an exit plan:

1. Is now a good time to sell the business?
2. Will the business stand up to due diligence?
3. Can the owner demonstrate growth prospects for the business?
4. Are the owner's financial expectations realistic?
5. What will happen to existing employees?
6. What will the owner and family do after the sale?

This chapter is set out in six sections, following the questions posed above. With the answers to these questions, the owner will be ready to draft an exit plan particular to his or her own business.

1. Is Now a Good Time to Sell the Business?

Timing a sale to maximise value for shareholders is one part of the challenge. The business must be ready, the marketplace must be hungry and buyers must be buying. When assessing the right time to sell a business, the following must be taken into consideration:

- **Market dynamics and conditions** Assess where the business is in the economic cycle and keep an eye on mergers and acquisitions (M&A) activity within your specific sector. Where you are in the marketplace will determine whether it is a buyer's or a seller's market.

- **Sell high** Sell at or near the peak of a cycle or rising market, when a valuation is at a level to generate a good return. Market dynamics and activity can boost a company's perceived value to a purchaser and thus present a window of opportunity. Some industries have a particular time when they do really well. Recruitment agencies, for example, are generally the first out of a recession and therefore become more valuable at a specific point in an economic cycle. The business must know *its* time through research and careful observation.

- **Consider what is driving the sale of the business** The best time to sell a business is when you don't need to. As such, if you are frequently approached about selling, consider doing so, as you could miss your opportunity; or, if the business is performing particularly well and you have decided to retire or relocate, the timing may also be right. Conversely, if personal circumstances dictate the sale during a less buoyant period, when the business is not performing well, the timing will be wrong.

2. Will the Business Stand up to Due Diligence?

In a report entitled "The Long Goodbye – Myths, realities and insights into the business exit process",[2] commissioned by Coutts & Co and based on research carried out in 2009, David Molian highlights that "only seven percent of businesses offered for sale attract a buyer – partly because they're marketed really badly and partly because there is no value in the business". This reinforces the key message that preparation is vital.

In difficult economic climates, people are seeking reasons or excuses *not* to do a deal, *not* to buy or sell. For that reason, due diligence is more onerous than ever before. Due diligence is the process through which a potential buyer evaluates a company or its assets before an acquisition. The buyer performs the investigation in order to get a clearer, more accurate picture about the state of the company it is seeking to acquire so that it can better evaluate the costs, benefits and risks.

---

[2] Molian, D., "The Long Goodbye – Myths, realities and insights into the business exit process" (Coutts & Co).

Readiness for sale is of critical importance and should be discussed by the company well in advance of the planned selling date. As well as being profitable and deemed valuable, there will be a variety of loose ends that will need to be tied up. These could include: health and safety matters; ensuring employee contracts are in place; ensuring supplier contracts are renewed on good terms and that the debtor book is in line with credit terms prior to marketing the business for sale. Essentially, the more planning that has gone into an exit strategy in the run-up to the sale, the less likely that a potential deal will collapse.

3. Can the Owner Demonstrate Growth Prospects for the Business?

For a business to achieve the best price possible, its value must be optimised and that value then convincingly validated for potential acquirers. "If you've got a well-run business, you've got to work hard on why your business is valuable and then you've got to sell that upside," says Brad Rosser, Sir Richard Branson's former right-hand man. "You've got to get it to the right stage and then prove it."[3]

While the balance sheet and profitability of a business can be key criteria for buyers (particularly financial buyers rather than trade buyers), historic profitability is quite likely to hold far less importance than the company's potential for *future* profitability and growth. It is equally likely that the buyer will add value by investing their own money, energy, customer contacts and product line into the business in order to augment its scalability. As such, there are many criteria that should be considered when grooming a business for sale to maximise its value, many of which have little to do with how much money it is making or has made in the past.

If a business owner can tick all of the following boxes, then the business is likely to achieve a good sale and command the best capital value possible:

- **A strong management team** This is vital. It's important to have not just a strong first layer but a strong second-layer

---

[3] Rosser, B., *Better, Stronger, Faster: Build it, scale it, flog it – The entrepreneur's guide to success in business* (Infinite Ideas, 2009).

management team. This will give buyers confidence that the company has people worth backing.

- **A robust succession plan and independent value** Management quality is vital in any instance, but particularly so if the owner intends to leave the company or step back from the MD role once the business is sold. Buyers must have confidence in any succession plan and in the chosen management team, while the business must have value independent of its owner to avoid owner dependency or over-reliance on certain individuals.

- **A scalable business model with a quality list of active clients generating regular income** Scalability can command a high valuation multiple. As well as having the capacity to grow in size and expand geographically, scalability is also about streamlining (to reduce the cost of sales as the business grows) while simultaneously generating recurring revenue.

- **Profitability and stability with effective cost and revenue management** Ideally, a business will be able to show that it has improved profits historically. However, future profitability is more relevant to buyers.

- **Realistic potential and strong prospects within a growth sector** There must be room for growth. It could be that you are number one in a market but don't have a very big company, in which case the market isn't very big and growth is likely to plateau if it hasn't already done so.

- **Reachable targets, particularly for the period during which the business is being evaluated** The selling process takes time. Therefore, if you're talking about target numbers, make sure that during the period you are in the view of the buyer you deliver whatever you say you'll do, and ideally better. Get it wrong and the buyer will lose confidence, because if you can't predict performance over a few months, how can you tell what will happen in a couple of years? It is not a good idea to miss targets consistently. If you do, the deal will most likely move from being a strategic purchase to a financial purchase, meaning you'll start talking about just the numbers; and once you start talking about numbers instead of the business, you lose value.

- **A strong brand and market position and the ability to clearly define your brand value proposition** Why do your customers choose your product rather than that of your competitors?

Put together a brand value proposition in a simple three to six-page storyboard, backed up with external validation. This can then be adopted by the buyer; your truth will be his truth. You should also examine the strategic reasons for the business existing in the way it does. Ask: if my business didn't exist, would I create it and in this form? Because if you can't make a coherent, *honest* statement as to why the business exists, then you're going to find it very difficult to sell.

- **A strong culture able to attract and retain talent** Motivated staff working within a communicative and unified culture are less likely to jump ship when the business is acquired.
- **All legal, accounting and tax 'paperwork' is in order** If not, this will slow down the sale process and could put off a potential buyer completely.
- **Competing offers** If there is interest from more than one party, the value will often be driven up. According to Stephen McGivern, "If you can run a controlled auction and have competition, either real or perceived, you tend to maximise the value."[4]
- **Good advisors focused on the key issues of managing the process and maximising value** Selling a business is not something you do every day, so external advice and help is important. Your professional advisor will not just find a buyer but should also create a process and structure to ensure that the business gets the best price *and* the best terms of sale. Most people find in retrospect that the sale of their business is far more emotionally demanding, stressful and time-consuming than they had anticipated at the outset. Engaging professional accountants and lawyers to manage the sale process not only maximises value, but also allows you to focus on running the business during the sale process.

4. Are the Owner's Financial Expectations Realistic?

When a business has created value, it will attract acquirers rather than having to go out looking for them. By building value within a certain

---

[4] McGivern, S. Interview with author. Stephen McGivern is Corporate Finance Partner at Hughes Blake Chartered Accountants.

sector, the firm will already be on the radar of potential buyers, and this will help to ensure that the right people make the approach. However, the most likely buyer may not always be the right buyer. Sometimes the person who is likely to pay the most is quite often the person the owner would like to sell to the least, as they have the most to gain from the sale, i.e. your biggest competitor. You don't necessarily want to talk to them; but if you do, you need to consider how and when to release detailed, confidential information about your business and its customers. Having said that, the company with the best reasons to buy your business will most likely to be well known to you.

In order to find the right buyer for your company, you need to carefully consider the strategic reasons why buyers may wish to acquire the business. Ideally, it's better to sell to strategic trade buyers who may place a higher value on what you can offer them. It's therefore crucial to determine exactly how you can make the business strategically attractive to the right buyer for the right price.

In terms of financial buyers, if there is no strategic reason for them to invest, they tend not to offer the best price because they're acquiring for a straight return on capital. Whereas if the buyer is a multinational that wants to add your business to its footprint in Ireland/the UK, which it didn't have prior to the acquisition, it will tend to pay more.

Just as people buy the same products for different reasons, companies may have diverse intentions for wishing to acquire the same company. Each company may place a different value on the future potential of the business or other intangible assets. For example, a trade buyer might have a strategic interest in owning a brand because they'll be able use it as a platform; whereas a financial buyer tends to be disciplined about focusing on the future profits and upside as opposed to being seduced by the brand itself.

How to Market the Business for Sale

Whether the approach comes from potential acquirers or not, it may be necessary to market the business as an acquisition target by getting in front of the right people. To do so:

- **Be proactive** You will know more about the business than your advisor. So while it's good to have an advisor on board as a conduit, you should stay involved and help to sell the business.

- **Be discreet** Announcing to all and sundry that you're selling your company is not a wise course of action, as public announcements create uncertainty for staff, customers and suppliers. It's far better to have a corporate finance advisor contact potential acquirers discreetly on your behalf.
- **Be savvy** Ask your advisor to send out a draft memorandum to the best potential buyers, offering them an early/non-competitive sale if they can offer a good price for the business.
- **Use advisors with a large network** who can cast a wider net, catch more potential purchasers and research who the buyers are in any given market across the globe, from Ireland to the Far and Middle East.
- **Look close to home first** Investors who have helped you to scale up the business may wish to buy it or know someone who would. Alternatively, consider whether your management team may be appropriate purchasers of the business and whether it could attract appropriate funding for a management buyout (MBO).
- **Build up your PR** A year before you begin to implement your exit plan, organise and run a PR campaign about the business so that target acquirers will remember who you are and what you do. This will help to build the company's profile.

Selling for the Right Price

While the family and owner will be hoping to boost the value of the company to get a high price, potential purchasers will seek to discount its value to keep the price lower. Negotiations on both sides should therefore be anticipated. In order to manage this and get the right price:

- **Get your advisor to manage the sale process and agree a strategy for sale** This includes strategically deciding who to approach, when to approach and how to approach. Owners may not be the best person to negotiate the sale of their own business and therefore professionals should be engaged.
- **Listen to the advisor** "Most businesses are valued in a very sophisticated way by corporate finance advisors who know what they're talking about based on experience, so you've got to listen to them," advises Stephen McGivern.[5] Use your advisors

[5] McGivern, S. Interview with author.

to negotiate, acting as a buffer between the parties. Be prepared to step in if there is a deadlock, but consult the advisor first.

- **Know what you want before you begin to negotiate** Agree a baseline price with your advisor and discuss the likelihood of achieving that target. Be prepared to walk away from the deal if your expectations aren't met.

- **Agree a timetable for negotiations** to prevent discussions stagnating, but be flexible. Don't set a deadline before the date of a buyer's board meeting, when the potential acquisition may be discussed.

- **Ask the purchaser to make an offer (rather than telling them what you are selling for)** Insist that they reveal their hand and put a stake in the ground before you do. Avoid revealing your price – if you do, they'll think it's a ceiling, not a floor.

- **Make sure your ceiling price is a 'win–win'** There must be something in it for all parties. Certainly negotiate to get as high price as you can, but don't be greedy and risk losing the deal as a result.

- **Negotiate a price to include future value** While you'll be offered a price based on what the company is worth today, try to push the price up based on future value.

- **Be transparent with the buyer and upfront about potential risk** Honesty in the early stages of a negotiation can prevent the deal falling apart later on. In fact, some advisors suggest that you reveal weaknesses, threats and any bad news first, as opposed to focusing on the company's strengths. After all, you can't hide anything from the due diligence, nor would you wish to. For example, if you waited until an offer had been made before you revealed the state of your run-down office, you could find that the buyer reduces their offer. But if you show them at the start, their initial offer will already have taken that into account and, as buyers tend to begin with their lowest price anyway, it allows room for negotiation in the right direction. Furthermore, revealing your weaknesses and what you *can't* do doesn't automatically reduce the value of the business. In many ways it makes the business an even greater opportunity for a buyer who can bring something to it and add value, e.g. through securing some larger contracts, or taking the business to the next level with a more professional management team. The potential for adding value is a key criterion for most strategic buyers.

5. What will happen to existing employees?

Part of a good exit plan is considering where everybody – family and non-family employees – will end up in the next stage of the business. For example, are they going to remain with the organisation when it is sold? And should the younger management coming up behind fill the gap in three years' time? Will they be ready? Or will the business need to look for successors externally? (See **Chapter 10** on succession planning.)

If you are selling to a private equity financial buyer, they will clearly need someone in place who's capable of running the business. It may be that the owner-manager takes on responsibility for finding someone to fill that role, either internally or externally. Alternatively, the buyer may choose to recruit someone themselves. In which case, they are likely to bring in the best and most expensive person based on an outstanding track record. These alternatives will need to be addressed before completing a sale.

The acquiring company may have its own succession plans. If you're selling your business to the most strategic trade buyer, within six to 12 months they may want their own people to run the company. While retaining the previous owner has its initial benefits, once an earn-out period or the handover is complete, the previous CEO may be surplus to requirements.

If that's the case, it's important to be clear on where leading executives will end up following the sale of the business. As such, it's important to gain reassurance from buyers about your future role – and this goes both ways. While the buyers should take into consideration what the founder of the company wants his or her future involvement to be, the owner-manager should also understand what the buyer wants and be flexible.

6. What Will the Owner and Family Do After the Sale?

Building and selling the business was challenging, but your goals provided focus and energy. There are post-sale issues that ought to be addressed pre-sale and incorporated into preparations for the exit plan. It is wise to include a section in the exit plan on how the owner/family envisages post-sale life. The key aim here is to manage and protect the wealth accrued by the sale of the business.

- Have you minimised your tax exposure on the sale?
- Do you need to think about a family trust?
- Are you maximising the returns on your cash?
- What about inheritance tax planning?
- Do you have a clear investment strategy?
- Is there scope for tax-efficient investment?
- Do you have the right advisors?

Whatever you do next, the mistakes and successes you have made during your journey on the road to growth will enrich your path and enable your decision making. In building and growing your own business, you have contributed to the economy and to your own wealth of wisdom. Whatever challenges you pursue in the future will benefit from all you have learned throughout the process of business cultivation and evolution.

Drafting an Exit Plan

It's a good idea to set time horizons and financial goals and ambitions for the business for the next three and five years, around which you build your exit strategy. Ask questions such as: if you were to sell, who would it be to? What sort of value are you looking to sell for? Are you currently in the right shape for selling? Are you making the right decisions that will make you more attractive to a buyer, for example if you internationalise?

Below are some key points to follow in drafting a good exit plan.

SUMMARY: GUIDELINES FOR A GOOD EXIT PLAN

- **Plan way ahead of the sale.** Half of the entrepreneurs surveyed in the Coutts & Co "The Long Goodbye" report underestimated the time it would take to sell a business by at least 12 months. Business owners frequently don't allow enough time. It can take between two and three years from the decision to sell to the actual sale taking place.

- **Know your potential acquirer(s) and their strategic needs, then groom the business to accommodate those needs.** It's wise not just to identify who might wish to buy your business, but also to know what their strategy is and how acquiring your business may help them to achieve their strategic objectives. Evaluate your potential suitors and the reasons why they may be interested in acquiring you. What would be the key driver: revenue? Profit? Extending their geographical footprint? Do your homework on them; where they are now, where they are heading and any areas where they're experiencing difficulties, as this could be where acquiring you may prove valuable to them.

- **Allow for significant effort.** Selling a business takes time and should be viewed as a full-time job. You need to give yourself a few years so that you can continue grooming and growing the business while also working to sell it.

- **Prepare properly and start gathering data and getting paperwork in order early on.** Transparency is vital. You need to make it as easy as possible for the buyer to carry out due diligence. Pull everything together, including leases, staff and customer contracts, integrated financials, business plans, assumptions and case studies into a virtual data room. Have that data in the right format so you can distribute it accurately and quickly, as and when required.

- **Talk to your advisors at an early stage.** They can help identify the improvements required to maximise the sale value. You should also seek advice on tax planning considerations well in advance of the sale.

- **Gather case studies and testimonials** that reflect customer satisfaction levels and the strength of your value proposition from a customer's perspective.

- **Outline what is important to you from the sale of the business.** Is it price and continuity of the business? Long-term security of the company? A clean and fast exit? Or paying less tax?

- **Outline in your plan exactly how you will groom the business** to get it into the best shape for exit and which vital characteristics you will need to focus on to make the business as attractive and valuable as possible; from optimising efficiency and creating a strong management team to increasing the future prospects of the business.

- **Consider how you are going to run the business during the sale process to ensure that you continue to trade well and hit targets.** A frequent problem that businesses up for sale face is that, during a period when they are trying to sell the business (and impress buyers), they tend to see a real dip in the company's trading performance. So don't take your eye off the ball. You don't want potential buyers to think your business is in decline when it isn't.

- **Balance costs and investment appropriately.** Plan and forecast how you will curtail spending to operate at optimum efficiency during the exit phase (e.g. two to three years), while also ensuring that appropriate investment is made to feed forecasted growth and generate sufficient funds to excite the marketplace.

SUMMARY

Nine Steps to Becoming a Successful Family Business

By now you should have a very good understanding of the family business model – its advantages, disadvantages and best practice guidelines. It should be clear, too, that when a family and a business mesh productively and positively, it can create a thriving and sustainable business that can be passed down through the generations. The other side of that coin, of course, is the warning note sounded by the statistics set out previously: one in three family businesses fails within the first three years; less than 30% of family businesses make it to the second generation; and only 10% of those succeed to the third generation. Family businesses are not just important to owners and their families; as a sector the family business is hugely important nationally and internationally. This means it is imperative that owners, family members and staff work together to ensure they are equipped to confront the obstacles and challenges they will inevitably face.

It would be useful now to enumerate the key points that have been set out in this book, to leave you with a framework for your research, thinking, planning and the hard work to be done in your family business.

Figure: Nine Key Steps to Becoming a Successful Family Business[1]

```
                              9. Practising stewardship
                          8. Transferring ownership and control
                       7. Creating governance mechanisms
                    6. Strategically aligning the family and business
                 5. Sharing power across generations
              4. Practising communication and conflict resolution skills
           3. Building a shared vision and family team
        2. Becoming a learning family
     1. Becoming aware of family business challenges
```

[1] Carlock, Randel S., *Becoming a Learning Family: Tools for Growth and Development of Effective Business Families* (University of St Thomas College of Business Center for Family Enterprise, 1999). Quoted in Leach, P., *Family Businesses: The Essentials* (Profile Books, 2007).

The Nine Steps to Success in a Family Business

1. **Each family member must be aware of the challenges facing the business.**

   This is about fully understanding the make-up and challenges that affect the family business specifically (see **Chapter 1**). It's not enough to join the business and focus on day-to-day activities; each family member must research the family business and inform themselves by reading up on current trends, theories and best practice. This will ensure that they are capable of contributing to discussions on strengths and weaknesses, strategy and problem solving. Every serving family member needs to be clued in to the 'big picture' of the business from the start and never lose sight of it amidst the minutiae of daily demands. This is a special and ongoing responsibility and there should be continual review of the business and its achievements and losses.

2. **The family must work together to acquire the knowledge and skills necessary for making the business a viable enterprise.**

   The entrepreneurs interviewed for this book again and again stressed the benefits of incoming family members gaining knowledge and work experience elsewhere first, which they can bring with them in their role in the family business. No family member should be allowed to simply join – everyone wanting a role in the business should identify that role in advance and then go out and get the qualifications or skills needed to fulfil it to the very best of their ability. Serving members must stress the need to be a top-class professional in order to secure a place in the business. Serving members must also think about what skills the business may need in the future, and then ensure that those needs will be met. This is an ongoing process of education and skill set building for the greater good of the business, and as such it should be built into the family and business strategy documents (see point 6. below).

3. **The family must work together on a vision statement that guides every level of the business.**

   As set out in **Chapter 3**, the family must treat the creation of the vision statement very seriously and give it due consideration.

The vision statement will set out the family's view of where they want the business to go, how it will conduct itself in its dealings, how staff members are expected to behave and be treated and how success will be achieved. As such, the vision statement consolidates the family's position and gives voice to the future vision for the whole company, creating a realistic framework for longevity. Of course, it's not enough to simply draw up the document – it must be 'lived' by every staff member, every day and in every aspect of the business.

4. **Practise good communication, including how to resolve arguments effectively.**
Good communication is a vital skill for all businesses. Confrontation and conflict are inevitable, and the perfect solution isn't always clear in every situation, so communication and conflict resolution require mindful and skilful handling to ensure positive outcomes. **Chapter 3** set out the role and nature of communication in the family business, with advice on how to set up and conduct workshops to help develop good communication and conflict resolution skills and procedures in the family business.

5. **Ensure that power is shared across the generations working in the business.**
Incoming family members must be brought into the fold to ensure they fully understand the dynamics of the business, their role within it and the future roles they may wish to hold. It is entirely unhelpful to restrict power and decision making to a few individuals and treat everyone else as being on a different footing or a lower rung on the ladder. An open and welcoming enterprise that demands a high level of professionalism and contribution from each family member will ensure that those family members step up to meet expectations, raising their game in the process. It also demonstrates a commitment to future succession. **Chapter 8** considered how to engage the next generation.

6. **Create a strategic plan that aligns family and business needs and ambitions.**
The business should always be looking to the future, to new opportunities and chances to grow, which means a strategic plan that

shows how the business will grow, and how the family members will grow with it, is a very useful document. **Chapter 6** set out the nature and parameters of the family constitution, a policy document that creates a shared vision and a shared ambition between the family and the business. It is part of creating an overarching strategy that aligns the family's needs and ambitions with those of the business, now and into the future. It should also help to ensure that potential problems in the family don't negatively affect the business and vice versa.

7. **Devise and implement corporate and family governance structures and policies.**

   As highlighted in **Chapters 5** and **6**, governance structures and policies are essential to the family business. These frameworks allow for transparency in all dealings, ensure power is shared across the generations and provide guidelines to staff (both family and non-family) for how to work individually and together. It is time-consuming and requires lots of discussion and debate, but those are healthy things for a business and will present a clear path for the business – and the family – to follow. That kind of clarity is crucial for the business, and it further ensures that the highly sensitive issue of succession will not be the death of the business.

8. **Draw up a comprehensive succession plan with input from all family members concerned.**

   This is often the hardest policy to implement because it is where emotions and professional ambitions can mix, sometimes with negative results. This need not be the case, however, if the family works together early to produce a detailed, fair and transparent succession plan that describes processes, deadlines and the expectations of everyone involved. By turning succession into a professional, structured process, the emotional impact on the owner/founder and his or her family can be lessened. Succession is as inevitable as death and taxes, so the family must pull together to create a process and a plan that facilitates a smooth and positive transition that does not undermine the business. **Chapter 10** provided a step-by-step guide to setting up and enacting a comprehensive succession plan.

9. **Draw up a stewardship document and ensure that it informs all aspects of the business.**

   Effective stewardship is about passing on a healthier, more successful business than the one you inherited, which is the ultimate aim of every family member who believes in and works in the family business. This is again about the family discussing the small and big pictures together and distilling their ambitions, hopes and strategies into a coherent, well-communicated statement of the vision and values of the family and business. It is important to draft a stewardship declaration, where asset management, dividend distribution, succession and financial planning and the obligations and responsibilities of family members are all defined and set out. When people can see the path clearly, they are more likely to embark on the journey and see it through to its successful end.

Index